GOOD NEWS STUDIES

Consulting Editor: Robert J. Karris, O.F.M.

Volume 27

The Kingdom
of
God in History

by

Benedict T. Viviano, O.P.

Michael Glazier
Wilmington, Delaware

About the Author

Benedict T. Viviano, O.P. is currently a professor of the New Testament at the Ecole Biblique, Jerusalem, and dean of studies at the Ecumenical Research Institute, Tantur. He is the author of *Study as Worship: A Commentary on Matthew,* and has been published in the *Catholic Biblical Quarterly,* the *Journal of Biblical Literature* and *Spirituality Today,* among others. As well, Father Viviano has served as an associate editor of the *Catholic Biblical Quarterly,* and is currently associate editor of the *Revue Biblique.*

First published in 1988 by Michael Glazier, Inc., 1935 West Fourth Street, Wilmington, Delaware 19805.

Library of Congress Catalog Card Number: 86-45329
International Standard Book Number: 0-89453-600-1

Typography by Laura Burke.
Printed in the United States of America.

For my brother Paul,
d.1984

TABLE OF CONTENTS

INTRODUCTION

The impulse to write this book came from two sources. On the one hand, as a teacher of New Testament literature, and particularly as an interpreter of the synoptic gospels, it early became obvious to me that the central theme of the preaching of the historical Jesus of Nazareth was the near approach of the kingdom of God. Yet, to my amazement, this theme played hardly any role in the systematic theology I had been taught in the seminary. Upon further investigation I realized that this theme had in many ways been largely ignored in the theology and spirituality and liturgy of the church in the past two thousand years, and when not ignored, often distorted beyond recognition. How could this be? On the other hand, as a responsible Christian teacher, trying to relate the biblical message to contemporary concerns, especially to the emerging greater concern in the churches for social justice, both at home and in relation to the Third World, I also realized that the best New Testament basis for such concerns was precisely Jesus' proclamation of the kingdom of God. In a word, the kingdom was of explosive power, if only it was fully understood.

Had the church willfully tried to suppress the message of the kingdom, or had she simply misunderstood it? Had it simply become lost in the shuffle as Christians moved from an apocalyptically charged Palestinian culture to a Hellenistic Stoically influenced culture where the chief values advocated were inner serenity even for slaves (Epictetus) and an enlightenment of soul which led to union with the One in a blissful spiritual eternity beyond this vale of tears (the Hermetic literature)? Or had the church simply suffered an apocalyptic burn-out, as a result of too many shattered hopes and bitter failures? (After all, something like this happened to the Jews for a long while.) Moreover, the element of government intimidation could not be ruled out then or now. For example, it is easier to understand how the parish priests failed to preach the center of the Christian message when we realize that as late as in the 18th century in "Catholic" Austria the sermon topics for Sunday services were set by the government office for church affairs, and that every book checked out of the university library by a theology professor was reported to the secret police. Something like this is going on in many countries today. And yet government intimidation cannot account for everything in this story, as we shall see. In brief, what happened to the kingdom of God in history?

As I tried to find out the answer to that question I realized that there was room in English for a short book which would tell the story through some of its major representative figures. A selection was necessary. Inevitably the author is not equally familiar with every period of Christian history. Nor did he feel competent to provide a chapter on the roots of the theme in the ancient Near Eastern concept of kingship. What follows then is a combination of biblical theology and the history of ideas which will, I dare to hope, also provide part of a theological basis for Christian involvement in the struggles for justice in the world.

There is clearly a need for a work of this kind in English. There exist two works in German which attempt to tell much the same story. One is by Johannes Weiss, *Die Idee des Reiches Gottes in der Theologie*, a book of 156 pages published in 1901. It provides a model for my work and it would be good to have it in English, but it omits the medieval part of the story and could not tell what happened between 1901 and 1984. The other work is on a completely different scale. Ernst Staehelin of Basel spent a lifetime compiling interpretations of the kingdom of God from the Fathers of the Church to modern times. His collection of sources was published in seven stately volumes from 1951 to 1965 under the title *Die Verkündigung des Reiches Gottes in der Kirche Jesu Christi.* The reader who wishes to pursue the matter further will find this ample work a gold-mine.

There is also a standard short work in English, Karl Löwith's *Meaning in History.* Written by a professional philosopher, this book traces the understanding of the kingdom of God in the great philosophers of history but avoids exegesis.

There are also related works on the history of millennarian thought, on the social teachings of the churches, on church-state relations, on the history of Christian doctrine, on the social world of early Christianity, on the theology of the land, on Christology and on the parables of Jesus, which cover some of the same ground. John E. Groh provides an excellent bibliographical survey in *Church History* 43 (1974) 257-267.

The specific focus of the present work will be on the kingdom of God in the gospels and on the interpretation of the kingdom and some attempts to realize it in later church history. It is obvious that the theme of the kingdom is comprehensive by nature and difficult to confine within a narrow compass. Only its importance can justify the effort.

The specific audience for this survey would be theological students and other readers with a minimum of theological education.

I would like to thank the following for the opportunity to present some of the ideas in this book for discussion: the University of Dubuque Seminary, Wartburg Seminary, Aquinas Institute, the priests' study groups of the arch-dioceses of Denver and St. Louis, the New England province of Assumptionists, and the social justice commission of Dominicans in North America under its outstanding leader Edward van Merrienboer. I must also thank the editor of the *Thomist* for permission to reprint some of the material in chapter three, and especially Nancy Hardesty for typing the manuscript.

St. Louis and Jerusalem 1987
The Feast of St. Matthew

1. THE KINGDOM OF GOD IN THE PREACHING OF JESUS

It is often remarked that the prophetic literature of the Old Testament provides a better basis for social justice concerns than does the bulk of the New Testament. On the face of it this seems palpably true. Paul is concerned with the inner life of his young ecclesial communities which he identifies with the body of Christ. John too seems chiefly to be concerned with love of the brethren and is apparently content to ignore or condemn the rest of the world. The book of Revelation does denounce the state grown demonic, but this book is too remote from the center of the New Testament, as this is understood by the mainline churches, for it to be suitable as the foundation stone for a New Testament social ethic. The charge with which we began would remain true were it not for the central theme of the preaching of Jesus, the kingdom of God.

Let us begin with some statistics. The term *basileia* (kingdom) occurs 162 times in the entire New Testament, 121 times in the Synoptic Gospels. The formula *basileia tou theou/tōn ouranōn* (kingdom of God/of the heavens) occurs 104 times in those gospels, in the distribution: Matthew 51 times, Mark 14 times, Luke 39 times. This distribution is high, and along with the content, justifies considering the formula a theological theme.

If we turn now to a single gospel, that of Mark, we can quickly get an idea of the manner in which Jesus employed the concept. We find it as the theme of his first public preaching:

> 'Now after John was arrested, Jesus came into Galilee, preaching the gospel of God, and saying, "The time is fulfilled, and the kingdom of God is at hand: repent, and believe in the gospel"' (Mark 1:14, 15).

(We will return to this verse later.) It is the content and purpose of the parables (4:11, 26, 30). It is the goal of death and the motive for ethical practice (9:1, 47). It must be approached as a child and is far from the rich (10:14, 15, 23-25). One who knows that the Great Commandment is to love is near to it (12:34). The Eucharistic meal anticipates it and looks forward to it (14:25). The man who takes care of the body of Jesus is one who seeks the kingdom (15:43). In brief, we may say that the kingdom of God is the ultimate horizon of the preaching of Jesus, ultimate both in the sense of value and in that of time and eternity.

What is the meaning of the phrase kingdom of God in the preaching of Jesus? He nowhere gives a definition and so there must remain an element of uncertainty and even of mystery about it (Mark 4:11), since he preferred to speak about it in parables. And yet we are not left wholly without resource. We must call to our aid the Old Testament, Jewish apocalyptic, rabbinic and targumic literature, and a single lucid verse from Saint Paul. But first we should take a closer look at the programmatic verses, Mark 1:14, 15.

Mark 1:14 makes two points. It begins with a definite time reference ("after John was arrested"), and it labels the preaching of Jesus as the gospel of God. These two points then become the frame for the next verse. "The time (*kairos*) is fulfilled" suggests that a major turning point in the unfolding of salvation history has been reached, a particular moment in time which inaugurates a new eon.

Behind this conviction lies the Jewish apocalyptic view that history is not simply an endless repetition of the same cycles, but is moving forward under God's guidance toward a goal. As it moves, it passes through various stages or eons. These are variously enumerated but a common periodization of history is into six ages: from Adam to Abraham; from Abraham to Moses; from Moses to David; from David to the Exile; from the Exile to the Messiah, who then inaugurates the final age. Alternatively the periodization can be based on the succession of world empires: Assyrian, Babylonian, Persian, Greek, Roman. (These lists vary from author to author. The important common elements are that history is moving toward a goal and that the process is under God's care and guidance; in other words, history is not purely random or cyclical, it is not meaningless).[1]

Mark 1:15a is asserting that people are ready for another stage because the time is "full", that God is ready because the presuppositions are now there (cf. Gal 4:4), and that this new stage is inaugurated by the arrest of John the Baptist and by the public ministry of Jesus. The verse closes (15b) with a command to believe in the gospel. This means that the preaching of Jesus and God's inauguration of the final era are objects of faith (with a strong admixture of hope) not of sight, and that the appropriate human response is trust.

Now we move to the center of the verse: "the kingdom of God is at hand; repent." Jesus chooses to refer to the new eon as the time when the just and holy God of Israel will reign upon earth so completely that this new eon may simply be named the kingdom/rule of God. His will toward justice and holiness will in this eon be realized as perfectly on earth as it is in heaven. Confronted with this divine démarche the obvious initial human response must be repentance for past injustices, and a new turning to the will of God.

One problem remains. It is the interpretation of the tense of the verb "is at hand" (one word in Greek, *ēggiken*, from *eggizō*). The translation just given is deliberately ambiguous. If we analyze the verb further we can arrive at two rather

---

[1]D.S. Russell, *The Method and Message of Jewish Apocalyptic* (Philadelphia: Westminster, 1964), pp. 224-229.

different translations: (1) the kingdom of God is come, that is, has (already) come. This takes the perfect tense of the verb as referring to a past action with continuing *present* effect, and is the view of C.H. Dodd.[2] (2) The kingdom of God is coming, that is, it has drawn near; it is close at hand, but it has not yet arrived. It must still come in the near *future*. This view (that of J. Weiss and A. Schweitzer)[3] also takes the perfect tense of the verb as referring to a past action with present effect, but the past action in question is not *arriving* but drawing near, *approaching*. This is what the verb *eggizō* really means. Dodd can only defend his position by a reference to Matthew 12:28 and its parallel Luke 11:20: "if it is by the Spirit of God that I cast out demons, then the kingdom of God has come (*ephthasen*) upon you." Here the verb is *phthanō*, not *eggizō*, and *phthanō* really does mean *come*.

We are confronted here by a genuine difficulty. But it is not insurmountable. The verb in Mark 1:15 does mean "is near", not "has arrived". That this future expectation is the dominant motif in the preaching of Jesus will be clearer in what follows. For the time being we refer to the general apocalyptic framework and background of this verse which we have already set forth, and to the prayer which Jesus taught his disciples to pray. There (Matt 6:10) we are taught to pray "thy kingdom come, thy will be done", that is, we ask for *future* blessings, to come. What then of Matthew 12:28? The common explanation, which seems satisfactory to us, is that, in view of the context of that verse, demon-exorcisms, Jesus is saying that his wonder-working activity is a sign that God is active in history with power, that God is inaugurating a new era of history which has as its immediate goal the kingdom of God, that this kingdom is present in germ, sign

[2]C.H. Dodd, *The Parables of the Kingdom* (London: Collins, 1967; 1935), chapter two, pp. 29-61.

[3]J. Weiss, *Jesus' Proclamation of the Kingdom of God* (Philadelphia: Fortress, 1971); A. Schweitzer, *The Quest of the Historical Jesus* (New York: Macmillan, 1969).

and person in Jesus, even though its full socio-political realization has not yet occurred. Thus J. Weiss and his followers are correct in holding that the basic time reference in the message of the kingdom is future, as in the programmatic verse Mark 1:15, but that occasionally Jesus senses its present reality in sign and anticipation.

Although the Old Testament never uses the expression kingdom of God (except in Wisdom 10:10), the conviction that God, the God of Israel, is king is basic to it from one end to the other. This divine kingship means that he is lord of his creation, that he has in sovereign freedom chosen out of his humanity a particular people with whom he has chosen to make a covenant, like the oriental sovereigns with which the Israelites were familiar. As divine sovereign he is just and the administrator of ultimate justice and those whom he has chosen must serve him not only or chiefly by sacrificial cult or poetic hymn but by a justice corresponding to his. This is the message of the prophets and of the law of Israel. Deuteronomy instructs the judges of Israel: "Justice, justice shalt thou pursue" (Deut 16:20). In early apocalyptic this divine sovereignty is handed over to the Son of Man to bring down and to establish on earth (Daniel 7:13, 14), and this vision was decisive for the thought and deed of Jesus.[4] In rabbinics and in the later apocalyptic the Son of Man is identified with the Davidic messiah and linked up with the political and dynastic hopes of Israel, a combination of religious and nationalistic goals so tainted with destructively utopian and vengeful elements that Jesus had to distance himself from them.[5] But in the meantime, in the ordinary village synagogue liturgies, a curious thing was happening.

[4]J.J. Collins, *Daniel* (Wilmington: Glazier, 1981). esp. pp. 69-84, 130-145 and the literature there cited, to which add: John Gray, *The Biblical Doctrine of the Reign of God* (Edinburgh: Clark, 1979).

[5]J.J. Collins, "Patterns of Eschatology at Qumran," in *Traditions in Transformation* (eds. B. Halpern and J.D. Levenson; Winona Lake, IN: Eisenbrauns, 1981), pp. 331-373; B.T. Viviano, "The Kingdom of God in Qumran Literature," in a forthcoming volume edited by Wendell Willis, *The Interpretation of the Kingdom of God* (Boston: Hendrickson).

As Hebrew ceased to be intelligible to the ordinary Palestinian Jew, the Scripture lessons, after they had been read out in Hebrew, were then paraphrased in the popular tongue, Aramaic. These paraphrastic translations were later written down and called targums, that is, translations. One of the tendencies of these translations is that they try to avoid anthropomorphic characterizations of the Deity and try to avoid making God the subject of an active verb. To accomplish these goals they developed little reverent turns of phrase and "buffer words". Thus, instead of saying "God reigns", they would prefer to say "the Kingdom of God is here". Doubtless Jesus learned the expression Kingdom of God from his boyhood attendance at synagogue and naturally connected it with the kingdom (or kingship) which is handed over to the Son of Man in Daniel 7.

Now we know something about the origin of the phrase but still, what of its meaning? Strangely, the closest the Bible ever comes to a definition is found where, by all rights, it should not be found, in Romans 14:17. "The Kingdom of God does not mean [ritually proper] eating and drinking but justice and peace and joy in the Holy Spirit." This verse is usually misunderstood to refer exclusively to private, individual, interior, purely spiritual blessings such as a righteous standing of the individual before God, peace of mind and heart due to forgiveness of sins, the joy of a redeemed child. But, while those blessings are not to be excluded, they do not exhaust or even do full justice to the message of these words. After all, peace means primarily the opposite of war, the tranquillity of order, social order; justice means justice, the virtue proper to all social relations; and joy, although it has an individual dimension to it, can mean a rejoicing precisely in the blessings brought by peace and justice. These blessings may be taken to embrace the totality of all the goods of high civilization, e.g., the freedom to know the truth, to worship the truth once known, to cultivate all the arts and sciences in its service, to pursue the goals of society, family life and economics through free discussion and cooperation. Although stating it in these terms runs the risk of anachronism, this is a reasonable modern statement of the content of the message of the kingdom. Some further questions can however be clarified from the scriptures, namely, where is the kingdom to be realized, when will the kingdom come, who will bring it into existence, and what can we do about it?

Where is the kingdom? It is clear from the vision in Daniel 7 which is taken up into the New Testament that the kingdom originally is with the Ancient of Days, the heavenly Father, but when it comes it comes down to *earth*. Thus the kingdom is a this-worldly reality in its final realization, even though its origins are transcendent. This is not a common view among Christians, many of whom identify the kingdom with heaven itself and understand it as our individual and collective goal when we die. Purely heavenly, mystical and spiritual ideas of the kingdom find their basis primarily in Luke 17:20, 21 and in John 18:36 where Jesus says: "My kingship is not of this world: if my kingship were of this world, my servants would fight, that I might not be handed over to the Jews; but my kingship is not from the world." This common RSV translation gives the casual reader the impression that Jesus' kingship has nothing to do with this world but in fact the Greek text shows that it has no other meaning than the common synoptic doctrine, since the Greek preposition is *ek*, meaning *from*. Thus the verse should read: "My kingdom is not *from* this world," etc. That is, it does not come from here, does not originate here, but this leaves open the possibility that it could *come* here, a possibility which is directly taught and prayed for in the synoptics. We must here also mention as misleading Matthew's pious tendency to change the formula kingdom of God into the reverentially indirect kingdom of (the) Heaven(s). To him and his Palestinian Jewish readers it was obvious that this meant the kingdom of God (come down here on earth), but to later Gentile readers it has come to mean simply heaven. Thus Jewish pious circumlocutions intruded into the act of translation and when misunderstood, led to dangerous overspiritualizatons of basic biblical concepts. (Only a discriminating knowledge of the targums can deliver us from this kind of misunderstanding.)

When will the kingdom come? What is clear in this

difficult question to which the scriptures give in a sense different answers is that for the whole biblical witness the kingdom is an eschatological (that is, end-time) gift of God, which is not directly constructible by men. The question that remains is whether this gift has already been given to us in Jesus (present) or is still to come with the Son of Man (future). This is the basis for the scholarly debate concerning realized versus future or apocalyptic eschatology, a debate which has raged for almost a century now, with battle lines shifting back and forth. The present author believes that the key to this question is given in the Lord's Prayer (Matt 6:10), in which we are taught to pray: "Thy kingdom come." It would not be necesssary to pray this if it were already present. When Jesus says: "The Kingdom of God is at hand" or more literally "draws near", this does not mean that it has come already in its fullness but that it is imminent. Still the basic assertion is that it is coming in the near future. Further clarification on this comes from the next question.

Who brings the kingdom to earthly realization? In Daniel 7 it is clearly the Son of Man. In the gospels the answer is not so clear, since in them there emerges the problem of the Son of Man and his relation to Jesus. Traditionally it has been thought that Jesus identified himself with the Son of Man and that at his second coming in glory he would bring the kingdom. Today this view is fraught with difficulties. A close look at Mark 8:38 and the next verse, Mark 9:1, gives the impression (1) that although Jesus assumed a close, indeed decisive, connection between himself and the Son of Man the two are not clearly identical; (2) that there is a connection albeit not explicit between the coming of the Son of Man "in glory of his Father with the holy angels" and "the kingdom of God come with power."[6] Thus we must conclude

[6]Philip Vielhauer has denied any connection between the Son of Man and the Kingdom in Mark but his negative conclusion leads nowhere. The Danielic background of the two concepts makes their total separation in Mark improbable. P. Vielhauer, "Gottesreich und Menschensohn in der Verkündingung Jesu," in his *Aufsätze zum Neuen Testament* (Munich: Kaiser, 1965), pp. 55-91.

that there is an uncertain element in the earliest sources. To emerge from this dilemma we may choose to follow the path laid down by the final redactors of the gospels, and by the book of Revelation. In that case we would say that the kingdom is inaugurated by Jesus as sign, anticipation (prolepsis) and foretaste, and this sign, anticipation and foretaste are continued by the Holy Spirit and the Church, until the kingdom is brought definitively by the Son of Man, himself personally identical with Jesus, as risen Lord.

Drawing together some lessons from this first section we may say that the kingdom of God in the preaching of Jesus is a social, and not primarily or exclusively an individual, interior, spiritual, reality. The sign that it is present in its fullness will be justice on earth, that is, the elimination of the grosser social evils. This is the realization of God's reign on earth.

What can we do about the kingdom? According to Matt 6:10 we must pray, "Thy kingdom come". We conclude from this that the kingdom is a divine, transcendent reality whch is truly God's and is therefore not *directly* constructible, much less controllable, by man. This is an important point because in the course of history many people have identified the kingdom of God with their own favorite political or ecclesiastical project and this overly close identification inevitably leads to disillusionment and despair and often to catastrophe. We must be careful therefore to maintain a distinction between our efforts and the definitive gift of God. No human political program, no matter how important or how fine, can be simply identified with the kingdom of God. But still the question remains: what are we to do about it? Clearly we are to pray for it as for the greatest of God's gifts. This is the first point, never to be neglected. We must long for it, we must "hunger and thirst for justice" (Matt 5:6). Beyond this we can get a clue from the rabbis which also finds an echo in the New Testament. The rabbis said that good deeds, especially when they are performed by the whole of Israel, *hasten* the coming of the kingdom. Thus Rabbi Levi (ca. 300) declared: "if the Israelites observed one

Sabbath as it should be observed, the Son of David would come immediately" (y. Ta'anit 1, 64a).[7] When the early Christians were becoming anxious about the delay of the Parousia, the author of Second Peter wrote them a letter of encouragement and advice and used the rabbinic expression "hastening the coming (parousia) of the day of the Lord" (2 Peter 3:12). We may assume that the author had the same idea as the rabbis, that is, we do not directly *construct* the Day of the Lord or his kingdom, but we can *prepare* (Matt 3:3) for it by prayer and by creating the groundwork or human presupposition for it, that is, a more and more perfect approximation to its high ideal. We can *hasten* the Parousia.

Ultimately the way we state the relationship between our role in the coming of the kingdom and God's role in it is going to be similar to the general solution we give to the classic theological problem of the mutual relationship of God's grace and our free response in faith in the total process of our salvation. Both are necessary. But God and we are not equals. His role is primary and sovereign. He has already taken the initiative in Jesus Christ. It is also his task to bring in the kingdom in its fullness. But he will not force it on an unwilling and an unready people. Our task in the times between is to remove obstacles, to prepare the world for the kingdom.

Thus we can see how the theme of the kingdom does provide a theological basis for social justice concerns and action on the part of Christians, in that it points to a realm of divine justice here on earth. Yet the kingdom as we have explained it is not to be identified with any purely human program, even though these can and must prepare for and hasten it. It remains in God's hands. But Christians must remain restless and discontent until the full measure of God's plan has come to fulfillment. Thus Christians should be straining forward with hope and longing and earnest prayer,

[7]Rudolf Schnackenburg, *God's Rule and Kingdom* (New York: Herder and Herder, 1963), pp. 60-62; 85-86.

but also with their intelligence and plans and actions. All this may not be building the kingdom but it is *preparing* for it.

What we have said so far is largely biblical theology, based on Mark and Q-sayings, that is, on the earliest strata of the gospel material. We have proceeded in this fashion in order to get as close as possible to the views of the historical Jesus, to touch the hem of his garment, so to speak. To round out our picture of the gospel material it will be well, without trying to be exhaustive, to present some special aspects of the message of the kingdom which are found only in Matthew and in Luke.

Turning first to Matthew, we focus on two special emphases. These are his peculiar link-up of eschatology (judgment) and ethics, and his concern about the church. The first of these themes is not unique to Matthew's gospel. It is present in all the gospels, but it receives more thorough treatment in Matthew. The second theme, the church, is found explicitly only in Matthew, although Luke handles it in Acts, and John treats it in his own highly symbolic way (vine and branches, sheep and sheepfold).[8]

The link between the kingdom and ethics is found in two different forms in Matthew. It is first found in direct statements such as "Seek first his kingdom and his *righteousness* (justice), and all these things shall be yours as well" (Matt 6:33). That the kingdom is of top priority and connected with the struggle for justice is very clear from its position as the first and last reward in the beatitudes (Matt 5:3 and 10). Verse 10 is especially striking in this regard: "blessed are those who are persecuted for righteousness' (justice's) sake, for theirs is the kingdom of heaven." The second form in which the link is found is in parables. There

---

[8]G. Bornkamm, in Bornkamm-Barth-Held, *Tradition and Interpretation in Matthew* (Philadelphia: Westminster, 1963; 1960), pp. 15-51; G. Bornkamm, "The Risen Lord and the Earthly Jesus: Matthew 28:16-20," in *The Future of Our Religious Past*, ed. J.M. Robinson (London: SCM, 1971), pp. 203-229; J.D. Kingsbury, *The Parables of Jesus in Matthew 13* (Richmond: John Knox, 1969); Armin Kretzer, *Die Herrschaft der Himmel und die Söhne des Reiches* (SBM, 10; Stuttgart-Würzburg: KBW-Echter, 1971).

is a series of seven parables of the kingdom in Chapter 13, structurally the center of the gospel. There is another grouping, a trilogy of parables, in Matt 21:28 - 22:14. But the greatest parable of the kingdom and its connection with ethics is the beautiful and powerful judgment scene in Matthew 25:31-46, the parable of the sheep and the goats.

> "Then the king will say to those at his right hand, 'Come, O blessed of my Father, inherit the kigdom prepared for you from the foundation of the world; for I was hungry and you gave me food, I was thirsty and you gave me drink, I was a stranger and you welcomed me, I was naked and you clothed me, I was sick and you visited me, I was in prison and you came to me.'" (Matt 25:34-36)

The answer of the righteous and the fate of "those at his left hand" are both well known. It is not that Matthew is legalistic or lacking in compassion for sinners. What he is concerned about is to warn Christians against complacency and to encourage them to live their faith. Their fate in view of the kingdom depends upon it.

The second special feature of Matthew with respect to the kingdom is his assertion of a link between the kingdom of God (coming in the future) and the presently existing church. It has become a cliché in theology since Loisy that Jesus announced the kingdom but what came instead was (unfortunately?) the church. It is true that the band of disciples which Jesus had gathered around him during his time on earth became what was called a church after his death. Traditionally the church is said to be born from the pierced side of Christ, or, alternatively, it is said that she is born at Pentecost. Peter and Paul then in the post-Easter period become the great founders of churches (Gal 2:7, 8). At first glance Acts and Paul seem to speak little about the kingdom but much about the church. What then, the question may well arise, is the connection between the church and the kingdom? It is this question to which an at least partial answer is given in the famous "Thou art Peter" passage in Matthew (16:17-19; cf. 18:17, 18). Much has been written about this passage which is not our concern now. We have only to consider a single point, the relation between kingdom and church. Consider the words:

> " 'And I tell you, you are Peter, and on this rock I will build my *church*, and the powers of death shall not prevail against it. I will give you the keys of the *kingdom* of heaven, and whatever you bind on earth shall be bound in heaven, and whatever you loose on earth shall be loosed in heaven.' " (Matt 16:18, 19)

These words then assert that there is a connection between church and kingdom, that leaders in the church hold the keys to the kingdom, and, implicitly, that our relationship to them has some bearing on our relationship to our eternal destiny. The church is not the kingdom, nor is it heaven, but it is the path to them, a gathering of those who look toward them.

Our treatment of Luke will be brief. Let us begin with some statistics of Lucan usage. Of the thirty-five mentions of the kingdom of God in his gospel, eight are parallel with both Mark and Matthew, eleven parallel with Matthew alone (Q), one with Mark alone, fifteen are proper to Luke's gospel. In addition there are seven in Acts. Thus there is both a traditional element in Luke and an innovative element. Of the 35 + 7 occurrences in Luke-Acts, 21 + 2 are cases where the kingdom is future, 2 + 0 where it seems both present and future. Thus the future aspect is more frequent in Luke, as it is in the other synoptic gospels. But there are other cases where the kingdom is in some sense *present*, twelve cases in all. In part these are parallel to what we have seen in the earliest stratum of the gospels. Thus Luke 11:20 parallels Matthew 12:28 (quoted on pp. 16). There are also some genuinely new elements, partly in the form of suggestive silences and replacements. We will only consider two such cases, found in chapters four and seventeen of Luke.

In 4:16-30 Luke begins his account of the public ministry of Jesus with a magnificent scene, Jesus' first preaching in the synagogue at Nazareth. Jesus fulfills Isaiah's prophecy of liberation and announces salvation to the Gentiles. Not for nothing is this a favorite text of missionaries, catechists, and theologians of liberation. But there is also a problem lurking here. This scene is Luke's equivalent to Mark 1:15 (= Matt 4:17) which we have already studied. Yet there is no announcement of the near approach of the kingdom. There is an eerie silence on this point. The kingdom is displaced by a quotation from Isaiah 61:1, 2; 58:6:

> "The Spirit of the Lord is upon me, because he has anointed me to preach good news to the poor. He has sent me to proclaim release to the captives and recovering of sight to the blind, to set at liberty those who are oppressed, to proclaim the acceptable year of the Lord."

One could hardly ask for a better description of what the kingdom of God come to earth would mean. This *is* the kingdom. Why then does Luke not mention it? We will have to proceed carefully here. There can be no doubt that Luke was convinced: where Jesus is, the kingdom is near. Moreover, from the viewpoint of contemporary needs for a biblical basis for social action we can judge Luke's substitution of an Old Testament quotation for a mention of the kingdom as in some respects more vivid and helpful. Yet we must fault him for not giving expression to this central theme of Jesus' proclamation and hope in the terms which were in a special way Jesus' own. Others had spoken of the kingdom before him, but no one had centered everything upon it in the way he did. Luke has here failed to present Jesus in his uniqueness and in the fullness of his eschatological expectation. In a word, his text is politically richer but theologically poorer. The best thing would have been to show how the Isaiah text elucidated the kingdom hope. Perhaps this is what is meant when the text adds: "Today this scripture has been fulfilled in your hearing" (Luke 4:21).

The second case we must consider is Luke 17:21b: "The kingdom of God is in the midst of you." Here is clear teaching that the kingdom of God is present in the saving power and healing work of Jesus. As such it is in line with early, likely authentic sayings such as we have seen in Matthew 12:28, paralleled in Luke 11:20. In context, and this is important, this saying introduces a whole discourse on the eschatological coming of the Son of Man (Luke 17:22 - 18:8). Thus the *present* intervention of the kingdom is only a beginning. It remains to be accomplished. Those who can recognize the presence of the kingdom in the ministry of Jesus are invited to turn themselves toward its completion.

Understood in this way, the saying does not undermine the essential futurity of the kingdom hope and makes perfectly good sense, as a subsidiary but legitimate aspect of the total picture. Unfortunately the verse has been abused throughout history and led to an overly spiritual, de-politicized and thus trivialized interpretation of the kingdom. First, it is a mistake to make this verse the starting point of our understanding of the kingdom in the proclamation of Jesus. More programmatic verses (such as Mark 1:15) must be the basis. Secondly, on the strength of this verse it would be illegitimate to understand the kingdom as a "purely religious blessing, the inner link with the living God."[9] Of course it is a religious blessing, it is a link with God. But it is also God's way of addressing our social, political, earthly needs, of asserting his rights and his will for justice over his creation. A purely private, withdrawn spirituality is not a kingdom spirituality.

There is one final feature of Luke's handling of the kingdom theme which is peculiar to his work and which we may profitably consider. There are seven plus five passages (Luke 4:43; 8:1; 9:2, 11, 60, 62; 16:16; Acts 8:12; 19:8; 20:25; 28:23, 31) having the character of general summaries where the kingdom of God is presented as the *object of preaching*, the direct object of the verbs *euaggelizesthai* (to announce the good news), *kērussein* (to proclaim), *diaggelein* (to announce), *diamartureisthai* (to bear witness to), and the

---

[9]A. Harnack, *What is Christianity?* (New York: Harper, 1957; 1900), p. 62.

like. These passages are quite general, even vague, as to when or how the kingdom will be realized concretely. Some authors understand the kingdom in these cases as meaning the Christian Church, others as Christian preaching and teaching, but many others as the eschatological reign of God. Probably the best understanding of the matter is that while in these cases the kingdom does refer to the future reign, in the Gospel at least, there is also a strong concern that the preaching of the kingdom contain an appeal to the hearers to make a *present* decision of faith. But that the kingdom is central and the ultimate goal of the early Christian mission becomes magnificently plain in the very last verse of Acts (28:31) where Paul is in Rome, the heart of the Empire, "preaching the kingdom of God and teaching about the Lord Jesus Christ quite openly and unhindered."[10]

Let us frankly recognize that biblical exegesis cannot solve all of our contemporary theological or ethical problems, nor should we ask it to provide us with specific political programs. But the biblical message of the near approach of God's kingdom can point us in the right direction. For example, it teaches us to expect more to happen in this world, in this life, in this time and history, by God's saving power. God has not finished with his humanity. There is more to hope for. Moreover, if this first point be true, if God still takes this old, nearly exhausted world seriously, then we must take this world seriously too. We have to concern ourselves with more than even heaven or hell. (But this does not mean that we should deny or be uninterested in eternal life or the faith in the resurrection of the body, because in any case we must all die or somehow pass from this life to be with God.) Thirdly, the kingdom hope should lead us to engage in the struggle for justice and for a more humane social order, for world peace and for universal disarmament. Our engagement in this struggle can be without illusion because we know by faith that no human program by itself will bring in the eschaton. Our engagement can also be

---

[10]A. George, *Etudes sur l'oeuvre de Luc* (Paris: Gabalda, 1978), pp. 285-306.

without ultimate despair, because we believe that, no matter how great our self-created horror becomes, God is faithful to his promise and he will bring in the kingdom which has already drawn near us in his Son.

To re-enforce and to clarify our presentation of the kingdom from the viewpoint of systematic theology it will be well to close with a list of four characteristics of the kingdom drawn up by a theologian who suffered exile from his native land on account of his political engagement, Paul Tillich.[11] The kingdom is political, it is social (that is, it includes peace and justice without which there is no true holiness), it is personalistic, giving eternal meaning to the individual person, and it is universal, embracing all men and women and the entire cosmos. These really are essential components of the kingdom, which is not pie in the sky by and by but God's future for humanity.

To Tillich's list we must add from our exegetical and theological study that the kingdom is a gift of God which achieves the realization of justice and love, peace and joy (Matt 6:33; Rom 14:17). It will be earthly, territorial, in space, time and history, when it comes in its fullness (Dan 7:13f; Matt 6:10). It is still to come in the future but is present by anticipation in Jesus and the Spirit. It is brought by the Son of Man and in this sense is an aspect of Christology.[12]

To attempt to define the indefinable, we could say that the kingdom of God is a future apocalyptic divine gift not built by human beings directly but given as a response to hopeful prayer, longing and hastening struggle. It is the final act of God in visiting and redeeming his people, a comprehensive term for the blessings of salvation, that is, all the blessings secured by that act of God.

[11]P. Tillich, *Systematic Theology, III* (Chicago: University of Chicago Press, 1963), p. 358f.

[12]Norman Perrin, *The Kingdom of God in the Teaching of Jesus* (Philadelphia: Westminster, 1963).

2. THE KINGDOM OF GOD IN THE CHURCH FATHERS

Since the kingdom of God is a great biblical theme, it is a force which has energized and transformed the lives of people and communities. One of the best ways to understand the full implications of such a theme therefore is to observe its effects in the continuing life of the church. This constitutes the theme's *Fortleben* or "afterlife."

If we continue to tell the story of what happened to Jesus' message of the kingdom in the time after his earthly ministry, we can only do so selectively. Our survey will include the Apostolic Fathers (the earliest successors of the New Testament authors), Justin, Irenaeus, Cyprian, Origen, Hilary of Poitiers, Eusebius, Augustine and the founders of the Holy Roman Empire.

But before we enter into particular authors, it might be well to sketch out the main lines of development schematically, so that we can have an overall view.

There are four main currents of interpretation and realization of the kingdom of God in the history of Christianity from the close of the New Testament canon to the year A.D. 1000, and indeed these currents continue in various ways down to modern times. The first is the eschatological stream which is a continuation of the New Testament doctrine itself, already described in chapter one. The greatest representative of this stream is St. Irenaeus, bishop of Lyons. The second stream is the spiritual-mystical one, where the kingdom is identified either with some *present* spiritual good in the soul of the believer, like knowledge, contemplation, spiritual and intellectual illumination, or the practice of Christian virtue. Alternatively the kingdom may be identified with a *future* blessed state of the faithful, whether conceived as the general resurrection, immortality and corruptibility, or eternal life with God—in a word, heaven. An early major representative would be Origen.

The third main current is the political school. This view identifies the kingdom of God on earth with some political structure or program. The two great examples of this understanding are the Christian Empire of Constantine in the East (Byzantium) and the Holy Roman Empire of Charlemagne in the West. The first major theoretician and theological apologist for this view is Constantine's advisor, Eusebius of Caesarea, the father of church history.

The fourth view of the kingdom may be called the ecclesial school, because it identifies the kingdom of God on earth with the church, sometimes called the kingdom of Christ to distinguish it from the kingdom of God in heaven. This has been the most common view among Roman Catholics from the time of its first, cautious, proposal by St. Augustine in his massive work, *The City of God*, up to the middle of this century.

The reader will have noticed that the first two of these four currents remain in the realm of religious hope, faith, and teaching, whereas the second two connect the kingdom idea with actually existing human institutions. The full implications of this divergence are enormous in their working out but we call attention to it here merely to alert the reader that the story of what happened to the kingdom proclamation of Jesus involves two quite different aspects. One is in the nature of a history of ideas or doctrines, intellectual history. The other is in the nature of a history of social entities, states and churches, and is more like ordinary, political history. Although our account will have mostly to do with the intellectual side, the social will emerge as the result of the ideas, especially in this chapter. This may cause some confusion of genres and some puzzlement but it also reflects the fascination of this theme which stands precisely at the point of interaction of ideas and historical-social reality.

I. The Eschatological Stream

The reason the kingdom hope was lost so early in the history of the church is that this hope presupposes a late Jewish apocalyptic worldview such as we find in the book of Daniel. Once Christianity moved out of the sphere of Palestinian and diaspora Judaism into the Greco-Roman world the cultural presuppositions which could have made such a hope intelligible were no longer present. This was the price that Paul and the other early Christian missionaries had to pay for their success. The later church fathers did not know Judaism from the inside. Even when they knew of apocalyptic ideas they often found them incredible or pastorally unsuitable. Once Christianity came into close contact with Greek philosophy the problematic shifted away from the social salvation represented by the kingdom of God to issues of personal individual salvation: death, immortality of the soul, the attainment of eternal life.

But those early church fathers who remained outside of the philosophical outlook still kept alive the old hopes. The earliest Christian writers outside the canonical scriptures we call the Apostolic Fathers. We will give a few selected quotations from them.

The letter of Clement, commonly dated from Rome around A.D. 95, in an important section on the foundation of church order on the apostles, says that "they went forth in the full assurance of the Holy Spirit preaching the good news that the kingdom of God is coming" (1 Clem. 42:3). The future kingdom is the central content of their preaching, as it was for Jesus. In another place Clement says that "those who were perfected in love by the grace of God ... shall be made manifest at the visitation (*episkopē*) of the kingdom of God" (50:3). The use of the term *episkopē* in connection with the kingdom is a little unusual, but has New Testament analogues (Luke 19:44 and I Peter 2:12) and, even more important, is a frequent Old Testament term for God's gracious acts in history (Hebrew *pāqad*). This suggests how close Clement is to the biblical manner of expression and to its hope.

The author of an early Christian homily called Second Clement, dated plus or minus A.D. 150, keeps the kingdom hope alive and uses it as a motive for ethical conduct here and now: "If then we do justice before God we shall enter into his kingdom, and shall receive the promises . . . Let us then wait for the kingdom of God, from hour to hour, in love and justice, seeing that we do not know the day of the appearing (*epiphaneia*) of God" (2 Clem 11:7 and 12:1).

The earliest Christian manual of church order and practice is called the Didache or Teaching of the Twelve Apostles. Because of its many archaic features it is sometimes dated very early, even A.D. 50-70. In the form we have it may be dated a bit later, around A.D. 150. The kingdom is mentioned first in the transmission of the Lord's Prayer (8:2), then, twice, in the prayers for the eucharist: "As this broken bread was scattered upon the mountains, but was brought together and became one (loaf), so let thy church be gathered together from the ends of the earth into thy kingdom" (9:4; cf. 10:5). In chapter sixteen the full endtime hope of the early Christians is vibrantly alive but the term kingdom does not occur. Another early, related, document, the Epistle of Barnabas, contains an uncanonical saying attributed to Jesus: "those who will to see me, and attain to my kingdom must lay hold of me through pain and suffering" (7:11), a saying which may be echoed in Acts 14:22, and whose spiritual relevance needs no stress. Barnabas also has a hint of the ages of the world and the millennial hope (15:4,5).

The greatest writer among the Apostolic Fathers was Ignatius of Antioch, bishop and martyr. He wrote seven letters to various churches on his way to meet the lions in Rome, sometime between A.D. 108 and 117. Although close in spirit in many ways to Paul, he is closer still to John and thus understands the alternative to the "old kingdom" as eternal life and the abolition of death (Eph 19:3). His only awareness of the kingdom comes through two echoes of a Pauline verse: "Do you not know that the unjust will not inherit the kingdom of God?" (1 Cor 6:9, 10; Ign Eph 16:1; Phld 3:3). The same verse is cited by Polycarp, the martyred bishop of Smyrna, in his letter to the Philippians (5:3) written before his death in A.D. 155 or 156.

As a witness to the spirit of the second century martyrs we find a bold stroke in the account of Polycarp's death. When the anonymous author wants to fix the date of death he first gives the names of the contemporaneous high priest and pro-consul, but instead of the expected reference to the reigning emperor he pointedly inserts the phrase "but Jesus Christ was reigning forever" (Mart. Pol. 21). He knew the political implications.

A contemporary of Polycarp, Papias, bishop of Hierapolis in Asia Minor, wrote a treatise around A.D. 130, now lost, but reported on by Eusebius and Irenaeus. Eusebius records him as stating that "there will be a certain period of a thousand years after the resurrection from the dead, when the kingdom of Christ must be set up in a material order on this earth" (*Hist. eccl.* 3.39.12).

In their expectation of a thousand year duration of the kingdom, Barnabas and Papias were undoubtedly influenced by the millennial time frame set forth in the Book of Revelation (20:1-10). It is well to point out here that the eschatological understanding of the kingdom which we discerned in the Synoptic Gospels (see chapter one) has no such time frame. It does not exclude it, it simply does not mention it. It is our theological judgment that this time limit is not, and need not be, a central object of Christian faith and hope. Thus we are not promoting a form of millenarianism or chiliasm, doctrines of a thousand year reign of the saints. But we do think that the kingdom proclamation of Jesus is important for modern theology and belief.

The doctrine of Papias was developed still further in Irenaeus, the bishop of Lyons, traditionally thought to have met a martyr's end around A.D. 200.

> (The blessing of Isaac) refers unquestionably to the times of the (messianic) kingdom when the righteous shall bear rule, upon their rising from the dead; when also the Creation, having been renovated and set free, shall bring forth an abundance of all kinds of food (simply) from the dew of heaven, and from the fertility of the earth. The Elders who say John, the disciple of the Lord, related that they had heard from him what the Lord used to teach in regard to these times, saying: The days will come in which vines shall grow, each having ten thousand branches, and in each branch ten thousand twigs, and in each twig ten thousand shoots, and in each one of the shoots ten thousand clusters, and on every one of the clusters ten thousand grapes, and every grape when pressed will give five and twenty measures of wine. And when any one of the saints shall lay hold of a cluster, another shall cry out: 'I am a better cluster, take me; bless the Lord through me' (*Adversus omnes Haereses* 5.33.3).

On this view the kingdom will follow upon the resurrection (as in Revelation 20). What is new here is the renewal of the earth and its extravagant fecundity. Irenaeus is important for our theme not because of this extravagance but because he clings with undiminished intensity to a this-worldly hope coming from God. He has not lost this gospel element. (It will be quite different with the Alexandrian theologians like Origen.)[1]

We will conclude our documentation of this current with the thought of Justin Martyr (approximately 100 to 165). Justin wrote an apology or defense of Christian faith to the

---

[1]For further information on early Christian millenarianism, see Jean Daniélou, *The Theology of Jewish Christianity* (London: DLT, 1964), pp. 377-404.

Roman emperor Antoninus Pius and his persecuting son Marcus Aurelius. The situation was tense, his approach bold. Choosing his words carefully, he tells the emperor what kingdom Christians look for:

> And when you hear that we look for a kingdom, you suppose . . . that we speak of a human kingdom; whereas we speak of that which is with God, as appears also from the confession of their faith made by those who are charged with being Christian, though they know that death is the punishment awarded to him who so confesses. For if we looked for a human kingdom, we should also deny our Christ, that we might not be slain; and we should strive to escape detection, that we might obtain what we expect. But since our hopes are not fixed on the present, we are not concerned when men cut us off; since also death is a debt which must at all events be paid (1.11).

Christians look then for a future kingdom from God. Justin does not here go into more detail. To have said this was risky enough.

In another setting, at Ephesus, in his Dialogue with Trypho, a Jewish interlocutor, Justin is less guarded: "I, and all other entirely orthodox Christians, know that there will be a resurrection of the flesh for a period of a thousand years in a rebuilt Jerusalem, adorned and enlarged, as the prophets Ezekiel and Isaiah, and others affirm" (*Dial.* 80.4). Justin goes on in this full millennarian vein in succeeding chapters. Though he knows the philosophical schools, Justin has not abandoned early Christian endtime hope. Indeed, to Justin goes the honor of having clarified the two comings (*parousias*) of Christ, one in lowliness, the other in glory (*Apol.* 1.52.3). One problem of which Justin is an early example is that, for authors who know the roots of Jesus' kingdom message in Daniel, the temptation is great to refer to the kingdom as eternal (*aiōnios*), because Daniel says that the dominion of the Son of Man is an everlasting one (7:14; cf. 2 Pet 1:11). Justin does this frequently (e.g., *Dial.* 140.2).

The problem is that, precisely in trying to be faithful to an *apocalyptic* biblical text, they employ language which is open to a static, ahistorical, Platonizing distortion. Not only does this contradict a thousand year reign (which we do not need to defend), but it also makes it difficult to envisage any earthly realization of the kingdom, since nothing earthly is eternal. Only "eternity" is eternal, so that, if the eternity of the kingdom is emphasized, the easiest option is to say that the kingdom equals heaven, and this world is abandoned to its fate. The compromise solution to which we are attracted holds that there will be a temporarly limited (but unspecified) realization of the kingdom of God on earth, followed by a heavenly eternal reign.

As an appendix to this section we may note the beautiful meditation on the Lord's Prayer by St. Cyprian of Carthage, martyred in 258:

> Next we pray: 'Thy kingdom come.' Here we are asking that the kingdom of God be made present for us ... Surely there cannot be a time when God does not reign? What has always existed with him and will never cease to exist could never have a beginning. It is for the coming of *our* kingdom, then, that we are asking, that kingdom which was promised to us by God and acquired by the blood of Christ poured out in his passion. Before that, we were slaves in the world [actually Cyprian was of high social standing], but now we pray that *we* may reign under the sovereignty of Christ (*De orat. dom.* 13, emphases added).

Cyprian here oscillates between the eschatological and the spiritual approaches. But he also raises an important question: can there be a time when God does not reign? Of course the answer of faith is: no. The basic biblical assumption is that God is sovereign lord of his creation. In this sense he always reigns, his kingdom always exists. But: his creation has fallen from him. In Christ he is gradually reasserting his lordship over his fallen and now in principle redeemed creation.[2] This faith also explains a puzzling feature of the Beatitudes (Matt 5:3-10). In them all the reward clauses are in the future ("for they *shall* see God") except the first and last ("for theirs *is* the kingdom"). Why the kingdom in the present tense? Cyprian gives the answer: God is always reigning. It would be irreverent to deny this. The problem is that his rule does not yet extend fully to earth, to us.[3]

II. *The Spiritual-Mystical Stream*

As Christianity made the great cultural transition for the Jewish, Palestinian, Semitic and apocalyptic world of its origins to the surrounding imperial world of Greco-Roman classicism with amazing speed, due to the extraordinary missionary dynamism of Paul and to the bold theological streamlining of the gospel according to John, there was inevitably loss and gain. The gain was that Christ was proclaimed to the known world, and was often accepted as revealer and savior; that Christianity ceased to be a rejected Jewish sect and became a world religion (or at least an empire-wide mystery religion); it became catholic. The main loss was of the apocalyptic dimension of Christian hope. The dual hope of the Christian, the kingdom of God and resurrection of the dead, (or at least of the saints), was reduced to the resurrection of the individual to eternal life in heaven. The social and the this-worldly historical dimensions of hope were lost.

This loss did not happen by accident. The Hellenistic philosophical mind (as opposed to the historical minds of Herodotus, Thucydides and Polybius) was primarily interested in the universal, the necessary, the eternal. This fits with Plato's mathematical bias and Aristotle's (pre-Dar-

---

[2]E. Käsemann, "The Righteousness of God in Paul," chapter seven in his *New Testament Questions of Today* (London: SCM, 1969), pp. 168-182.

[3]J. Dupont, *Les Béatitudes* (EBib; Paris: Gabalda, 1973) 2.116-123.

winian) biological interest. Scientific knowledge rested on the foundation of stable natures, eternal essences, static species. From this point of view history was meaningless, an endless cyclical recurrence, like the rhythm of the seasons. Since the world was eternal, history had no goal. Life was an end in itself. The only enemy was death. A religious message which promised eternal life, especially as understood as the immortality of the soul, could therefore be of great interest. But a message of a future divine intervention into history which would alter social structures in the direction of peace and justice was a bit too much to envisage (even though utopian thinking was not unknown to the ancients and Plato in his *Gorgias* has a kind of last judgment).

In any case many people in every age are mainly concerned about their own personal lives. Hence the perennial popularity of the spiritual-mystical interpretation of the kingdom, since spirituality represents the personal appropriation of Christian doctrine. (John Sanford's *The Kingdom Within* is a contemporary religious bestseller which interprets Matthew's gospel in Jungian terms as a "book of the soul.")

The great early Christian thinker, Origen of Alexandria (c. 185-c. 254), intended to follow in the footsteps of Paul and John in taking Christianity beyond the mental horizons of Judaism. He may also have wanted to follow his great Alexandrian predecessor, Philo the Jew, in trying to show how Moses predated Plato and taught him all that was valuable in his thought. Certainly he shared with Philo a preference for an allegorical meaning of history which turns out, upon closer acquaintance, to transform much biblical history into general moral truths of a philosophical cast. (This is so despite his theology of history and the central role he attributed to Christ.) A man of extraordinarily varied mental gifts, he may also have wanted to meet the challenge posed by his pagan classmate Plotinus in his neo-Platonic system-building.

In any case and for whatever reasons, he certainly wrought some bold changes in Christian eschatology. (Not content with transforming the kingdom doctrine, he also dissolved the Christian expectation of the resurrection of the body into the immortality of the soul, since Christian perfection consists, on this Platonizing view, in a progressive dematerialization).

In our presentation of Origen on the kingdom of God let us begin with two passages from his commentary on Matthew: "Or Christ is himself, the king of heaven, the kingdom of heaven, likened to a treasure hidden in the field" (Or. *Matt.* 10.5 (G.C.S., p. 6.1). "And as he is himself wisdom itself and justice itself and truth itself, so perhaps he is also himself the kingdom itself (*ho autobasileia*) . . . and if you want to understand the verse "theirs is the kingdom of heaven" you may say that theirs is Christ according as he is himself the kingdom (*autobasileia*)" (Ibid. 14.7 (G.C.S., p. 189.17). We see here the problem clearly. Origen is a clever man; he is a mystic, a religious genius, deeply imbued with a Johannine view of Christ as the way, the truth and the life. Why not carry the unifying tendency further and identify the kingdom with Jesus? (Some exegetes even see this as the meaning in John 3:3, 5, although that point is by no means obvious. There we read: "Unless one is born anew, he cannot see the kingdom of God . . . Unless one is born of water and the Spirit, he cannot enter the kingdom of God)." It is all so tidy, monistic and edifying. But of course all social, territorial, earthly, justice-oriented connotations are lost.

Origen has a famous treatise on prayer, much of which consists of a commentary on the Lord's Prayer. This treatise has had a great influence on spirituality and monasticism. For now we need to say something about its liturgical use.

In 1925, Pope Pius XI instituted the feast of Christ the King. He did so with a conscious religio-political intent. After World War I Europe faced a breakdown of political morality and the rise of unprincipled dictators. Pius XI had seen with his own eyes the Soviet rampage in Poland, had indeed been traumatized by it. As Pope he witnessed the rise of fascism in Italy and Portugal, the persecution of the church by leftists in Mexico and was soon to know the homicidal regimes of Hitler and Stalin. As a Christian leader he felt called to raise a protest in the name of Christ, to assert the "crown rights of the redeemer" against the willful brutality of men. By this idea-feast and its accompanying encyclical letter he reminded believers and statesmen of Christ's sovereignty over hearts as messianic redeemer king. The pope did not build his theology on an apocalyptic understanding of a future coming of Christ to reign on earth. But as far as it goes, his idea of a special feast in honor of Christ the King is a good one, and has been widely followed in other churches. This feast may be regarded as the patronal feast of this particular biblical theme. The reform of the Roman liturgy of 1970 has even given the feast new prominence by setting it at the very end of the church year, bringing it into contact with Advent's looking forward to the second coming of Christ. But, in the liturgy of the hours or breviary, the second reading is taken from Origen's treatise, the twenty-fifth chapter, which comments on the phrase Thy Kingdom Come and does so in a thoroughly spiritualizing-individualizing manner which weakens the potential force of the feast and is therefore to be regretted.

Although the chapter is too long to be quoted in full, we can give an idea of it. Of course Origen begins with Luke 17:21 "The Kingdom of God is within you" (see our chapter one thereon), and proceeds on that basis to interpret a veritable flood of kingdom texts in a purely spiritual, interior, private and realized sense. (His mastery of Scripture is remarkable.) Everything is made to speak of the perfection of the individual soul, attainable here and now, so much so that he must answer the objection: why pray for it to come if we have already attained it? His reply simply offers the hope of receiving ever "greater visions of wisdom and knowledge."

The essence of his thought runs: "By the kingdom of God, I believe, is meant the happy enthronement of reason and the rule of wise counsels; and by the kingdom of Christ, the saving words that reach those who hear, and the accomplished works of justice and the other virtues. For the Son of God is Word and Justice." If we try to read this sympathetically we can agree that the kingdom does have to do with reason, wisdom and justice. But Origen has missed any sense of historical development or movement toward a divinely intended social goal. The repeated phrase "in us" is the signature of his interiorization of the concept.

But Origen is not only a spiritual writer or exegete. He is also the great speculator of the *apocatastasis* or restoration of all creation (Acts 3:21). In his great exploratory work *Peri Archon, On First Principles*, Origen's doctrine on eschatology is scattered into several chapters distributed in three out of the four books. Many of his most controversial ideas, especially his suggestion that in the end, after due purgation, all sinners, even Satan and the other fallen angels, will be saved, we do not need to discuss, except to point out that they tend to flow from his union of Plato and Christ, in this case, the Platonic stress on unity and spirit as among the highest values. Having everyone saved in the end appeals to the philosopher's perennial quest for a tidy unity. But the religious source of Origen's speculations on eschatology is firmly biblical. Indeed, the text which more than any other seems to dominate and to unify his thinking in this area, I Cor 15:20-28, is so important that it is worth considering for its own sake, as well as for its influence on Origen.

> But in fact Christ has been raised from the dead, the first fruits of those who have fallen asleep. For as by a man came death, by a man has come also the *resurrection* of the dead. For as in Adam all die, so also in Christ shall all be made alive. But each in his own order: Christ the first fruits, then at his coming those who belong to Christ. Then comes the end, when he delivers the *kingdom* to God the Father after destroying every rule and every authority and power. For he must reign until he has put all his enemies under his feet. The last enemy to be destroyed is death. "For God has put all things in subjection under his feet." But when it says, "All things are put in subjection under him," it is plain that he is excepted who put all things under him. When all things are subjected to him, then the Son himself will also be subjected to him who put all things under him, that God may be everything to every one.

The main reasons 1 Cor 15:20-28 is so important are that it purports to give the *order* of the endtime events, and it unites a discussion of kingdom with the theme of *resurrection*. In these matters it differs from the synoptic gospels which we discussed in our first chapter. Our concern there was with Jesus' own proclamation of the kingdom which seems to have been the main burden of his concern. Resurrection comes up in the gospels only in contexts where the kingdom is not mentioned. The two concepts are not systematically related. To be sure, Jesus shared the common Pharisaic hope of resurrection (already expressed in Daniel 12:2), but neither he nor the synoptic evangelists think these two beliefs through to a unified synthesis. Respecting this state of affairs, we have stressed that the Christan has two hopes, one horizontal - the kingdom, the other vertical - resurrection, without trying to relate them. In fact however the kingdom is not purely horizontal but a point of intersection between the forward movement of earthly history and the final divine intervention in social history. It stands on the border between the immanent and the transcendent. That is why so many great modern (Platonizing) theologians move it just over the border into the purely transcendent. Thus it is to be expected that thinkers would try to bring the two concepts into connection. Since there is no unity, whether in or out of the Bible, in this matter, we stress no particular theory, although what Paul seems to say here makes sense to us: first kingdom, then resurrection. Yet the opposite also has some merit, viz., personal resurrection immediately upon death for those who die before the end time (no *general* resurrection, no intermediate state), and the kingdom for those alive at the time of the final blessing.[4]

From this Pauline starting point we are not surprised to read in Origen "that the goodness of God through Christ will

<hr>

[4]For some of the Pauline options in a contemporary perspective see the useful examination by Pierre Benoit, "L'evolution du langage apocalyptique dans le corpus paulinien," in *Apocalypses et Théologie de l'Espérance*, ed. L. Monloubou (LD 95; Paris: Cerf, 1977), pp. 299-335; but see now the appendix to X. Leon-Dufour, *Life and Death in the New Testament* (San Francisco: Harper, 1986), pp. 282-298, on the intermediate state.

restore his entire creation *to one end*, even his enemies being conquered and subdued" (*Peri Arch.*, 1.6.1). He conceives eschatology as protology, a restoration of paradisiacal conditions. In this he stands in the line of Barnabas who uttered the great principle: "See, I make the last things as the first" (6:13). The salvation of devils and the damned he derives from 1 Cor 15: 25 "For he [Christ] must reign until he has put *all* his enemies under his feet." But there is another motive: "to one end." That is, the end must attain a perfect unity, with no distinction between damned and saved, "that God might be everything to everyone." This is Platonism in action, yet building on the Bible.

Origen definitely has an eschatology. He believes in an afterlife. He brings kingdom (as heaven) and resurrection into a unity. But resurrection swallows kingdom and immateriality swallows resurrection. The vertical prevails over the horizontal so that the latter practically disappears. With this powerful advocate the spiritual interpretation of the kingdom continues to attract adherents down to the present day, both the devout and the politically conservative.[5]

As an early example of the spiritual interpretation in the Latin speaking Western church we may look briefly at Hilary, Bishop of Poitiers (c. 315-367). As the "Athanasius of the West," he strongly opposed the Arians by affirming the full divinity of the Son. In his early commentary on Matthew he understands the kingdom as a future reality, heaven, which we will attain at the resurrection, when Christ returns in the *adventus claritatis* (the arrival of glory). But the kingdom is also a present reality to the extent that it coincides with the church, the body of Christ. These views merge in the basic view that it is Christ himself who is the

---

[5]A rich survey of the subject may be found in G.W.H. Lampe, "Some notes on the significance of *basileia tou theou, basileia Christou*, in the Greek Fathers," JTS 49 (1948) 58-73. There is a study by Martin Eckart of Origen's use of 1 Cor 15:23-28, *Das Verständnis von 1 Kor 15, 23-28 bei Origenes* (Augsburg: St. Ottilien, 1966). There is an older work by R. Frick, *Die Geschichte des Reich-Gottes-Gedankens in der alten Kirche bis zu Origenes und Augustin* (BZNW, 3; Giessen: Töpelmann, 1928).

kingdom ("Cum ipse sit regnum coelorum ..." (*In Matt* 12:17 PL 9:989). Since the heavens are the saints, he is the kingdom of the saints.

In his mature work on the Trinity, Hilary faces a particular problem, the *traditio regni*. The Arians, in their desire to show the ultimate subordination of the Son to the Father, had built an argument on 1 Cor 15:24-28. There Paul says that when Christ has delivered the kingdom to God the Father (this is the *traditio regni*), "then the Son himself will also be subjected to him." To the Arians this showed the inferiority of the Son and his eventual reabsorption in the paternal abyss. Hilary devotes a whole book (11) to this problem. Here the elect are the kingdom. At the end Christ will bring them to the Father. The end does not mean ceasing to exist or absorption but fullness of being in the Father for them, full equality for the Son. In this polemical perspective Christology and Trinitology take precedence over eschatology. The connection between the kingdom of God and the future of this world is lost to view.[6]

III. The Political Current

It is easy to imagine the astonishment of Christians, after two and a half centuries of intermittent, sometimes erratic, sometimes systematic, persecution to find themselves living under a Roman emperor who not only claims to have converted to their faith but who wants to turn the whole empire into a Christian empire. It is important to understand this point well. Constantine the Great (d. 337) may not have been the first Christian emperor. Philip the Arabian, emperor from 244 to 249, may have been a Christian privately, or at least was sympathetically interested. But in any case he did not trouble the empire with his beliefs. Nor was it Constantine's intention to outlaw non-Christian cults or to

---

[6]Gilles Pelland, "Le thème biblique du Règne chez saint Hilaire de Poitiers," *Gregorianum* 60 (1979) 639-674.

force everyone to be Christian. Rather, after the battle of the Milvian Bridge in 312 wherein he defeated his rival Maxentius, he first tolerated Christians and showed them imperial favor. His long-range policy was to make Christianity the main religion of the empire, and thus to unify the empire in a new way. To this end he must try to unite the Christian church to the secular state by the closest possible ties. Although this in itself should have aroused the suspicions and reservations of Christians, some at least were so surprised by the turn of events that they thought they saw in it the hand of God, the confirmation of their hopes, the fulfillment of biblical promises.

Among such enthusiasts for the new state of affairs was one of Constantine's ecclesiastical advisers, Eusebius of Caesarea (c. 260 - c. 340). In 335, on the occasion of the celebration of Constantine's *tricennalia*, his thirtieth anniversary as emperor, Eusebius pronounced a panegyric oration in praise of the honoree. Neither man had long to live (the same cannot be said for the ideas expressed on the occasion). Perhaps carried away by the solemnity of the hour Eusebius cites Dan 7:18 ("And the saints of the Most High shall receive the kingdom") in a context where it refers to Constantine's appointment of his nephews Flavius Delmatius and Hannibalianus as caesars (subemperors). In the florid Byzantine prose style of the period this could be pressed to suggest that Constantine was the Son of Man who had received the Roman empire as the kingdom of God on earth. Eusebius does not say as much but his use of Daniel leaves him open to such a conclusion being drawn from his words. Certainly both he and the emperor believed that the latter was about a divine work and had a special share in the divine logos. Eusebius plays on the titles appropriate to God and the emperor, leading to a "happy confusion": "The Almighty Sovereign ... displays him as an example of true godliness to the human race. And thus our emperor, like the radiant sun, illuminates the most distant subjects of his empire ..., as with far piercing rays of his own brightness; ... himself everywhere present, and observant of every event ... Invested ... with a semblance of heavenly sovereignty, he directs his gaze above, and forms his earthly government according to the pattern of that divine original, feeling strength in its conformity to the monarchy of God."

These reflections then pass over to a defense of monarchy as such as the best form of government, best because most like God himself. "And surely monarchy far transcends every other constitution and form of government: for that democratic equality of power, which is its opposite, may rather be described as anarchy and disorder. Hence there is one God, and not two, or three, or more: for to assert a plurality of gods is plainly to deny the being of God at all. There is one Sovereign; and his Word and royal law is one: a law not expressed in syllables and words ... but the living and self-subsisting Word, who himself is God, and who administers his Father's kingdom on behalf of all who are after him and subject to his powers" (*Laus Const.* 3.3-7; G.C.S. 7, p. 201f). This is genuine political theology of the classical type, with its roots in Plato and Aristotle.

The connection between the heavenly Anointed and the earthly empire is drawn ever closer: "By an indescribable power he [Christ] filled the world in every part with his doctrine, expressing by the similitude of an earthly kingdom that heavenly one to which he earnestly invites all mankind, and presents it to them as a worthy object of their hope. And in this hope our divinely-favored emperor partakes even in this life ... He may truly deserve the imperial title who has formed his soul to royal virtues, according to the standard of that celestial kingdom. But ... one abandoned to ... vices ..., however he may be deemed powerful through despotic violence, has no true title to the name of emperor" (*Laus Const.* 4.3; 5.1-2).

Some have described Eusebius' application of Scripture as singular and vicious, a curiosity of patristic exegesis. But it is much more than that. It is downright fateful, creating a church-state tradition that determined a millennium or more of history and still leaves its effects. Supported by such theory, emperors in the East, and, after Charlemagne's coronation in 800, in the West, went on to consider themselves for practical purposes as the head of the church on earth, as popes so to speak.

To be sure, they sometimes did much good and exercised their high office in respect to the church with restraint. Moreover, we should not suppose that every church father in Byzantium was a naive Caesaropapist. The more theologically and scripturally minded fought any confusion between divine and human authority and applied to imperial relations the lessons learned by the prophets from the experience of the monarchy in Israel.[7] Nevertheless a pattern was set. It continued virtually unaltered in the Eastern Church until the fall of Constantinople to the Turks in 1453. Even then the idea of the Christian Empire did not die in the East. The Eastern Orthodox world soon turned to the Grand Dukes of Muscovy. Taking the title Tsar (= Caesar) they declared Moscow to be the Third Rome. That project did not cease till the Bolshevik Revolution in 1917.

The West continued fitfully under the emperors of the East till the barbarian invasions definitely shattered Byzantine control. Then, after a period of confusion, the pope, Leo III, crowned Charlemagne emperor of the West on Christmas, 800. Thus began, in principle at least, the Holy Roman Empire in the West. (Later the Western Empire came to be called the Holy Roman Empire of the "German Nation," though it still included many other ethnic groups.) Though an empire was only seriously realized a century after Charlemagne under the Ottonian Saxon emperors, and was often too weak for its tasks, it continued as a political entity down to the great secularization under Napoleon, executed by the archchancellor of the empire, the archbishop of Mainz, Karl Theodor von Dalberg, in 1803, the abdication of the emperor Francis II comprising the final act in 1806. But, already in 1804, Francis had declared

[7]See Michael Azkoul, "Sacerdotium et imperium: the Constantinian *renovatio* according to the Greek Fathers," *Theological Studies* 32 (1971) 431-464; Sir Steven Runciman, *The Byzantine Theocracy* (New York: Cambridge, 1977).

himself emperor of Austria to match Napoleon's proclamation of himself as emperor of the French that same year. Thus a feeble continuity with the old empire continued in Hapsburg lands down to 1918. But meanwhile the Hohenzollerns of Prussia had been created emperors of a second Reich (kingdom, empire) by Bismarck in 1870. This too fell in 1918. But the idea of the empire was too powerful to die. Thus in 1933, Adolf Hitler, a romantic Austrian political dreamer before he acquired power, announced the Third Reich, that is, the third embodiment of the Holy Roman Empire, which, in Eusebian terms, is the kingdom of God on earth! This loathsome project ended in flames in 1945.

It is not surprising that after the Second World War German exegetes and theologians, like Schnackenburg and Küng, while fully realizing the centrality of the eschatological kingdom of God in the sources of revelation, were most reluctant to admit event the slightest political connection. For them, Jesus' kingdom is purely spiritual and religious. Biblically, such an ethereal view is not warranted. Experientially, given their experience of the Third Reich, it is perfectly understandable. Obviously, the Hitler experiment stands as a permanent warning and question mark against any over-politicization of the kingdom. It tells us how powerful and dangerous it can be. But full human and religious life cannot be lived without some engagement with both power and danger. This little peek ahead to the full consequences of our story has, we hope, helped to show us something of the importance and the delicacy of the theme.

So Eusebius' legacy of identifying, at least for practical purposes, the kingdom of God on earth with the Christian empire had a long life. What constituted its appeal? It rests on two very broad bases. The first is philosophical. One of the most characteristic tendencies of the human mind, and especially of the metaphysical mind, is the search for unity, a coherent, simple harmony amidst the diversity of life. In Plato's *Republic* we see this tendency thought through politically to suffocatingly totalitarian conclusions, including the banishment of poets. The king is the philosopher is the high priest. Such a unified ideal has never failed to attract admirers.[8] The second basis is that Eusebius united the greatest and most long-lived political reality and idea in European history with the Christian religion. He wed the Roman empire to the church. In so doing he gave the empire a new lease on life, and made the church share responsibility for maintaining public order and the state. Once formulated, the idea would not die.

A few further thoughts on this current may show some lights and shadows of the matter. (1) When the imperial ideal began to disintegrate seriously under pressure from the rise of nation states, the national sovereigns began to develop theories of the divine right of kings, amounting to Eusebian claims in miniature.[9] (2) It is ironic that this potentially totalitarian ideal, so easily supported by mono-theistic ideology, should have been erected by the very emperor who convoked the first ecumenical council, at his summer palace in Nicea, to define the doctrine of the Trinity, a doctrine whose political consequences logically undermine a unitary theopolitical state.[10] (3) It is difficult to know what to make of empires. Arnold Toynbee tries to organize history into twenty-one civilizations each of which attains the phase of being a universal state or empire. But this phase remains ambiguous in his evaluation. On the one hand, an empire is a high point of political and cultural success and heightened possibilities. On the other hand, Toynbee de-scribes an empire as a long coma. Perhaps the implication is that people can find the vastness of an empire stupefying, whereas the snug manageability of a smaller nation state unleashes more creative possiblities. Such thoughts however

[8]As well as, e.g., Karl Popper's fierce criticism, in *The Open Society and its Enemies* (London: Routledge & K. Paul, 1966), vol. 1 *The Spell of Plato*.

[9]J.N. Figgis, *The Divine Right of Kings* (Cambridge: University Press, 1914).

[10]See Jürgen Moltmann, *The Trinity and the Kingdom: The Doctrine of God* (San Francisco: Harper, 1981).

trail off into the undemonstrable.[11] (4) By forcing Christians to share public responsibility the political current, besides dragging Christians into regrettable escapades like misguided crusades and pogroms, also made Christians try to interpret their biblical ethics in practical rather than in purely utopian terms. They learned that it is not so easy to govern justly. But they also had a chance to put some of their better ideas into legislated practice. For example, Constantine himself humanized the criminal law and the law of debt, mitigated the conditions of slavery, made grants to support poor children, removed unfair taxation and made Sunday a public day of rest. All this constituted a kind of "reality therapy" for Christians. (5) Another ambiguous outcome of this current was the development of the ideal of Christian knighthood. This involved a fusion of military and Christian values, a project both noble and easily perverted. The height of this process was the development of military religious orders like the Templars, the Hospitallers, and the Teutonic Knights.[12]

Further understanding of the political interpretation of the kingdom of God can only come from a consideration of the last of the four types of kingdom interpretation, the ecclesial school, since, at least in the West, their developments become closely intertwined.

IV. The Ecclesial Stream

Our major representative of this position is St. Augustine, bishop of Hippo, Bône in modern Algeria (354-430). We

---

[11]Arnold J. Toynbee, *A Study of History*, Abridgement of volumes I-VI by D.C. Somervell (New York: Oxford, 1946), esp. pp. 436-441; 522-532 ("the coma of a universal state", p. 532); idem, Abridgement of volumes VII-X (New York: Oxford, 1957), pp. 118f.: "This World is a province of the Kingdom of God, but it is a rebellious province, and, in the nature of things [esp. original sin], it will always remain so."

[12]Desmond Seward, *The Monks of War* (Hamden, Conn: Archon, 1972); Hartmut Boockmann, *Der deutsche Orden* (Munich: C.H. Beck, 1981).

notice at once that he is born fourteen years after the death of Eusebius. By the time he comes to completing his *City of God* (425) the church had had about a century of experience of this "Christian empire." The bloom was off the rose. No matter how highly they esteemed the Constantinian achievement, many Christians could no longer regard it as the kingdom of God on earth. Of that they were now quite sure. But if so, then where was the kingdom to be found concretely?

Augustine's *City of God* is probably the longest single book ever written about the kingdom. Of course it is concerned with many other things besides that, including a theology of history.

According to a recent study, the structure of the whole work is derived from the old apocalyptic scheme of the ages of the world, usually counted as six, sometimes as four or seven.[13] For our purposes we need only note that Augustine was strongly influenced by neo-Platonic philosophy and had even read Plotinus and Porphyry in the Latin translations of Marius Victorinus.[14] This philosophy was highly spiritual and other-worldly, centered on the one and the eternal, treating the material and the historically contingent as inferior stages in the ascent of the soul to union with the one. Christian devotees of this philosophy lost no time in linking it with the Johannine theology of eternal life and resurrection. In this thought there was really no place for a future divine kingdom coming to earth. The whole point of salvation was to leave the earth, so that one could be alone with the alone. Augustine christianizes and socializes this view through describing happiness as the beatifying shared vision of God, but this only occurs in heaven.

Thus Augustine was attracted to the spiritual interpretation of the kingdom we have already seen in Origen.

---

[13]A. Luneau, *Histoire du salut chez les Pères de l'Eglise: La doctrine des âges du monde* (Théologie Historique 2; Paris: Beauchesne, 1964). The main passages in Aug. are *de civ. dei*, 16:43; 15:1 and 9; 12:12; 2:19 and 21; 20:19 and 23; 22:7.

[14]Aug. *Conf.* 7.9.13; 8.2.2. Cf. P.R.L. Brown, *Augustine of Hippo* (Berkeley: Univ. of California, 1967), pp. 88-114, esp. p. 93.

Indeed, ultimately, for Augustine, the kingdom of God consists in eternal life with God in heaven. That is the *civitas dei*, the city of God, as opposed to the *civitas terrena*. That is his basic view. But, unlike Origen, he lived in the Christian empire. He could not ignore its claims to theological attention. Again, unlike Origen, he was a Roman who shared the Latin outlook of practical administration. He had almost, as a layman, become a provincial governor. He did in fact spend thirty-five years as a provincial bishop in North Africa. He had to take the church seriously as an institution. Indeed, as bishop, he not infrequently called on the local governor to help put down the Donatist schismatics.

In the great Book 19 Augustine, basing himself on Cicero's *de Republica*, defines a people or republic as an assemblage associated by a common acknowledgment of right (justice) and by a community of interests. Drawing on the Roman jurists, he defines justice as that virtue which gives everyone his due. He then argues that the empire cannot govern the provinces without injustice. And, since there can be no true republic where there is no justice, he draws the revolutionary, indeed treasonable, only implied conclusion that the empire is not a true state. Within the context of his apologetic this means that the sack of Rome by Alaric (410) is not an endtime catastrophe or a defeat for God's plans. Within the context of our question, it means that Augustine refuses religious ultimacy to the Christian empire since it is not the kingdom of God (19:21). In 19:24 he changes the definition of a people from one agreed on justice to one agreed on the objects of their *love*. From this point of view the Roman and other states are true states, but, since their love is not for the true God, they are usually void of true justice.

It is in 20:9 that we find the answer to our question: where is the kingdom now? Augustine says that "the Church even now is the kingdom of Christ, and the kingdom of heaven." This time of the church on earth is the thousand year reign of the saints promised in Rev 20:1-10. Of course he realizes that in the Church on earth the wheat is still mixed with the weeds, that the church as it is now is not the church as it is destined to be in heaven "when no wicked person shall be in her." Moreover, he believes that there are some outside the earthly church who will be in the city of God in heaven.

This highly qualified answer Augustine believed to be truer than the practical alternative: the empire as the present kingdom of Christ. But he knew well the limits and the flaws of the actual church. Not everyone who came after was to be so careful.[15]

Henceforward Christendom would have two practical rival theories as to where the kingdom was on earth: the empire and the church. Augustine's view would dominate and become the normal Roman Catholic view down to our own times. It would grow and develop, sometimes into exaggerated forms, especially among clergymen and those laymen interested in resisting the emperor. The imperial view would prevail in the East, but also in the West, at those times when the Western empire felt strong and sure of itself and among those circles which cherished the ideal of the Christian empire under an anointed priest-king. Whenever the papacy grew weak or disorganized the old ideal would rise up as an alternative. Of course other ideals also gradually developed, such as the church being governed by councils frequently in session(but then the question arose: who would convoke the council, the pope or the emperor?). And free cities and mendicant orders and craft guilds were developing more democratic, participatory models of government. These models would begin to transform the entire problem, issuing for example in a free church kingdom of God on earth in New England and a European community governed neither by pope nor by emperor. But that is getting ahead of the story.

A papal form of Augustinian theology develops throughout the high Middle Ages as a counterweight to western imperial Eusebianism until a severe clash occurs in the investiture controversy. This controversy, over the claim of

[15]R.A. Markus, *Saeculum: History and Society in the Theology of St. Augustine* (Cambridge: University Press, 1970).

the emperor and other lay princes to invest bishops-elect with their symbols of office and thus to control them, in its narrow sense runs from 1059 to 1122 and has as representative figures Pope Gregory VII and the emperor Henry IV. The abbot Joachim of Fiore's thought (on which see the next chapter) is, among other things, an effort to break out of the impasse to which this conflict has led. Pope Gregory IX and emperor Frederick II continue the conflict in the 13th century.[16] This phase subsides only with execution of Conradin, last of Frederick's line, by a prince loyal to the papal cause, and with a new imperial dynasty, the Habsburgs, which makes it a keystone of policy to work in harmony with the Holy See.

The struggle drags on during the "Babylonian Captivity" of the church when the popes resided in Avignon as dependents on the French court, during the Great Western schism, and the rival councils of Basel and Florence. At the Reformation Luther hoped to win over the emperor Charles V to his cause but succeeded in winning only two of the seven prince electors of the empire (during his lifetime): Saxony and Brandenburg.[17] The kings of England and Scandinavia also joined his cause, Henry VIII claiming to be supreme head of the church in England. Within Catholic circles the battle continued under the labels of Gallicanism in France and Josephinism or Febronianism in Austria.

From a political point of view we could see the struggle between pope and emperor as an element in the growth of two-party parliamentary democracies in Europe. The French Revolution deposes both pope and monarch briefly but it is amazing how western countries only relinquish the Platonic idea of a unitary theopolitical state in this century. State

---

[16]Ernst Hartwig Kantorowicz, *Frederick the Second, 1194-1250* (New York: Ungar, 1957); T.C. Van Cleve, *The Emperor Frederick II of Hohenstaufen, immutator mundi* (Oxford: Clarendon, 1972). Kantorowicz's other works are also useful, especially *Laudes Regiae: A Study in Liturgical Acclamations and Medieval Ruler Worship* (Berkeley: U. California, 1946).

[17]Karl Brandi, *The Emperor Charles V* (London: J. Cape, 1954).

churches still exist. And the new pluralism has not always been accepted peacefully or enthusiastically. The church is generally freer but more privatized.

Our far too rapid survey of the four main types of kingdom interpretation, the apocalyptic, the spiritual, the political and the ecclesial, and their historical consequences, has, we hope, shown the enormous power the idea of the kingdom of God has both for good and for ill. The stakes are high no matter how we decide to understand it. The theme can be dangerous and explosive.

Our next chapter will illustrate this with a case which occurs within medieval religious and theological circles.

3. THE KINGDOM OF GOD IN THE HIGH MIDDLE AGES

The Middle Ages on the whole did not understand well the this-worldly future dimension of the kingdom of God. This was so due to three factors: a widespread ignorance of the apocalyptic Jewish background of this expectation, together with an acute Platonizing longing for the eternal, for a place outside of time and history. This is the first factor. To it we must add the Augustinian transformation of the kingdom into the church militant and triumphant, and lastly the imperial ideology of the Christian empire as the kingdom of God on earth.

This unclarity about a this-worldly future divine kingdom characterizes three of the giants of high scholasticism: Bonaventure, Thomas and Albert. But before turning to their thought we should notice the one striking exception to this general state of affairs, the prophetic movement associated with the name of the Calabrian abbot, Joachim of Fiore (c. 1135-1202). Although Joachim, so far as I can tell, did not directly reflect on the kingdom theme of the gospels, he did renew a this-worldly hope of a new period of salvation history, which he called a third *status* of the world, in which the works of the Holy Spirit would be brought to perfection and in which there would be no need for clergy since all the people would be living as pure contemplatives. It seems that Joachim himself presumed a continuity between the church of the second *status* and that of the third *status*, a continuity which would be firmly maintained by a perduring Petrine papal office.[1] (The first *status* was the regime of the Old Testament, of God the Father.)

This simple threefold scheme of history sufficed to fire the imaginations and to raise the hopes of many for a better future in this world. As such it had revolutionary and socially disruptive potential.

While we cannot pursue all the tangled trails of Joachinism through the Middle Ages we must mention briefly the scandal created by the eternal gospel promulgated by the Franciscan Gerard of Borgo San Donnino (the modern Fidenza) in 1254. In that year Gerard circulated a collection of three of Joachim's main works together with an introduction in which he drew the most damaging conclusions. Seven errors extracted from that *libellus introductorius* were condemned by Pope Alexander IV on 23 October 1255. These errors are: (1) that the eternal gospel which is identical with Joachim's teaching surpasses the teaching of Christ and thus the whole Old and New Testaments; (2) that the gospel of Christ is not the gospel of the kingdom and therefore does not build up the church; (3) that the New Testament must be as invalid as the Old Testament; (4) that the New Testament will only remain in force for the next six years, that is, until the year A.D. 1260; (5) that those who live beyond this time are no longer held to accept the New Testament; (6) that to the gospel of Christ another gospel follows, and another priesthood in place of the priesthood of Christ; (7) that no one is able in himself to instruct people about spiritual and

---

[1]On Joachim and his influence see M. Reeves, *The Influence of Prophecy in the Later Middle Ages* (Oxford: Clarendon, 1969); *eadem, Joachim of Fiore and the Prophetic Future* (New York: Harper, 1976); B. McGinn, *Apocalyptic Spirituality* (New York: Paulist, 1979), pp. 97-181; *idem, Visions of the End* (New York: Columbia, 1979), pp. 126-141, 158-167; H. deLubac, *Exégèse Mediévale*, vol. 3 (Paris: Aubier, 1961), pp. 437-558; *ibid.*, vol. 4 (Paris: Aubier, 1964), pp. 325-344; E. Staehelin, *Die Verkündigung des Reiches Gottes in der Kirche Jesu Christi*, vol. 3 (Basel: Reinhardt, 1955), pp. 119-171, 251-269; H. de Lubac, *La posterité de Joachim de Flore* (Paris: Lethielleux, 1979); *Gregorianum* 62 (1981) 393-5;63 (1982) 677-699.

eternal matters except he go about barefoot.[2] At the University of Paris this affair was blown up to huge proportions by the animosity of the secular masters, and particularly William of St. Amour, against the Mendicants, the orders of begging friars, the Dominicans and Franciscans especially. Gerard had made matters worse by identifying the three angels of the fourteenth chapter of the Apocalypse with Joachim, Dominic and Francis and explaining them as heralds of the third *status*. At the Provincial Council of Arles in 1263 the whole "pernicious doctrine" of the three *status*, as preached by the Joachites, was condemned, together with the writings of Joachim which were its foundation. In spite of these condemnations and of the failure of Gerard's hopes to materialize in 1260, his doctrine spread like wildfire among many friars, affecting even the generals of the two major new orders. This situation provided a real threat to the leadership of the church and a challenge to the greatest theologians of the Franciscans and Dominicans, Bonaventure and Thomas Aquinas respectively. This crisis also helps to explain the relative blindness of these great men to the centrality of the gospel theme of the kingdom of God. To be sure it is only a partial explanation, but it did leave its mark.

The response of the two doctors varied as vary it must, given the different situation of the two orders. Bonaventure had to try to meet the Joachites within his order halfway, to attempt a compromise, because the number of extremists was larger among the Franciscans and the danger of their going into schism was greater, and because the eschatological evalution of their founder Francis was nearly universal among them and was shared by Bonaventure himself. This solution Bonaventure attempted in his great *Collationes in Hexaemeron* (lectures on Genesis 1) which he gave at the University of Paris early in the summer of 1273 and which

[2]Original Latin in H. Denifle and E. Chatelain, *Chartularium Universitatis Parisiensis*, vol. 1 (Paris, 1889), p. 272. Cf. E. Benz, "Die Exzerptsätze der Pariser Professoren aus dem Evangelium Aeternum," *ZKG* 51 (1932) 415ff.

had to be left incomplete and unrevised due to his elevation to the cardinalate. In this work Bonaventure undertakes a fundamental treatment of the theology of history. It is the only work in which a leading scholastic theologian attempts a synthesis of historical symbolic thought (such as characterized Joachim's interpretation of biblical prophecy) with the conceptual-abstract thought of Scholasticism.[3]

Abbreviating Bonaventure's careful and complicated schemes drastically we can say that he did attempt to discern a pattern of salvation history, including an expectation of an ultimate flowering of the Church within history. He follows Joachim exactly in the expression of this hope by placing the seventh age between the destruction of Antichrist and the Last Judgment and by distinguishing it from the eighth age.[4] He also lists Francis as a member of the ultimate order, the *ordo contemplatium*, the *ordo seraphicus*, and gives him eschatological status as Sixth Angel of the Apocalypse (Rev 7:2) and as Elijah in his second coming. But he does not hold that the concrete, historical Franciscan order is this ultimate, seraphic order. It is only *cherubicus* and not *seraphicus*. This means that the present Order of Franciscans is not yet the true Order of Francis. Thus Bonaventure makes a distinction between Francis and Franciscanism.[5] By means of these distinctions Bonaventure tried to link events of his own day with an imminent eschatological future while at the same time preserving continuity with the existing church. He inherits from Joachim a this-worldly hope but firmly connects it with the return of the Son and the abiding validity of the New Testament. In this he was perhaps being faithful to

[3]Bonaventure, *Opera omnia*, 10 vol. (Quaracchi, 1882-1902), vol. 5, pp. 329-449. Alternate recension ed. by F. Delorme, BFSchMA, 8 (Quaracchi, 1934). Reeves, *Prophecy*, pp. 66f., 179-181. The fundamental analysis is by J. Ratzinger, *The Theology of History in St. Bonaventure* (Germ. orig. 1959; Chicago: Franciscan Herald, 1971).

[4]*Collationes*, Delorme ed., p. 185.

[5]Ratzinger, *Theology of History*, pp. 31-51.

the true meaning of Joachim himself but not to his radical successors.[6]

The attitude of Thomas Aquinas to the radical expectations of a third age of the church aroused by the Joachite movement is more abruptly negative. But before we look at Thomas' relation to Joachimism we should first consider his position in regard to our central theme of the kingdom of God, in order to see why the Joachite conflict is relevant. If one consults the standard index to the two Summae of Thomas[7] under the word *regnum* (kingdom) one will find almost nothing. While this disconcerting result is not entirely justified, as we shall see, it contains an important lesson. The fact is that Thomas Aquinas does not devote any significant portion of his principal theological enterprise to the kingdom of God, the central theme of the preaching of Jesus. This may be considered a serious weakness in the greatest doctor of the medieval Church. Our task is not to praise or to blame but to understand. Of course Thomas has a vast moral construction built around the theme of justice in his great *Summa theologiae*. And as a matter of fact Thomas does treat of the kingdom in his commentary on Matthew as well as in his *Summa theologiae*, in his commentary on the Sentences, in the *Quaestiones quodlibetales* as well as in the theological opusculum, *Expositio super secundam decretalem ad Archidiaconum Tudertinum*. But in all of these instances except for the first it is in a context of polemical interaction with the theology of history of Joachim of Fiore.

[6]Reeves, *Prophecy*, p. 180f.

[7]*Indices ... in Summa theologiae et in Summa contra Gentiles ...*, ed. C.S. Suermondt (Rome: Leonine, 1948); the older index to the complete works of Thomas, called the *Tabula aurea*, of Peter of Bergamo (Rome: Paulinae, 1960), p. 822, adds a few minor references which do not substantially alter the picture: *In Sent.* 4, d.49, q.1, art. 2, q.5, c.; 1-2, q.108, a.1, ad 1um; *In Sent.* 4, d.15, q.3, a-1, q.4 ad 1um; *In Rom.* 10, lect. 1; 11, lect. 1; 14, lect. 2. The picture which emerges from the new massive *Index Thomisticus*, ed. R. Busa (Stuttgart: Frommann - Holzboog, 1975), Sectio II, vol. 19, entry no. 69107 - a, - b, pp. 290-293, is certainly much vaster and more complex, but not significantly different from that already drawn.

In his day the subject was theologically sensitive and Thomas handled it with reserve.

We will now consider some of the kingdom texts from Thomas and then suggest some reasons why he remained so cool toward the theme and toward Joachimism.

In his commentary on Matthew where he cannot bypass this theme we get the impression of a certain amount of confusion. This confusion may of course be due to his secretary since this commentary is a *reportatio*, that is, unrevised lecture notes taken down by a student secretary, as opposed to a *dictatus*. His view (on Matthew 3:2) runs:

> The Kingdom of Heaven in the scripture may be understood in four ways. For sometimes it means Christ himself dwelling in us through grace; Luke 17:21: *The Kingdom of God is within you.* Here the Kingdom of Heaven is spoken of because by means of the indwelling grace the way of the heavenly kingdom is begun in us. —Secondly the Kingdom can mean Sacred Scripture itself; thus Matthew 21:43 says: *The Kingdom of God will be taken away from you,* that is, Sacred Scripture. It is called a Kingdom because its law leads to the kingdom. —Third, it refers to the present Church militant; Matthew 13:47: *The Kingdom of Heaven is like a net cast into the sea and gathering all manner of fish,* etc. Here it is called a Kingdom because it is founded and set up in the manner of the heavenly Church. —Fourth, the Kingdom of Heaven can mean the heavenly court; Matthew 8:11: *They shall come from the east and from the west, and they shall recline with Abraham and Isaac and Jacob in the Kingdom of Heaven.*[8]

Of these four senses the first is the familiar false start based on Luke 17:21 which becomes the basis for an

---

[8]Thomas Aquinas, *Super Evangelium S. Matthaei lectura,* ed. R. Cai (Turin: Marietti, 1951), on ch. 3, verse 2, par. 250. Cf. Maximino Arias Reyero, *Thomas von Aquin als Exeget* (Einsiedeln: Johannes, 1971).

individualist, private interior definition. The third and fourth, the kingdom is the church on earth and heaven after death, follow the usual Augustinian line. The second, which defines the kingdom as Scripture itself, can only be characterized as a rather remote, arbitrary equivocation.

A second, more familiar passage on the kingdom comes in the *Summa theologiae*, in one of its finest sections of biblical theology, the tractate on biblical law (I-II, qq. 98-108). In the subsection on the New Law of the gospel (qq. 106-108), in q. 106, article 4, is found the question whether the new law will last till the end of the world. Here the objections are all derived from Joachite or radical Joachite teaching and the fourth explicitly mentions the kingdom (of God). In the body of the article Thomas makes a distinction in terms of the *status mundi*, Joachite terminology:

> The state of the world may change in two ways. In one way, according to a change of law, and thus no other state will succeed this state of the New Law. For the state of the New Law succeeded the state of the Old Law, as a more perfect law a less perfect one. Now no state of the present life can be more perfect than the state of the New Law ... In another way, the state of mankind may change according as man stands in relation to one and the same law more or less perfectly ... Thus, too, the state of the New Law is subject to change with regard to various places, times and persons, according as the grace of the Holy Spirit dwells in man more or less perfectly. Nevertheless, we are not to look forward to a state wherein man is to possess the grace of the Holy Spirit more perfectly than he has possessed it hitherto ....

With respect to a promised age of the Holy Spirit advanced in the third objection, he scores an effective point:

> The Old Law corresponded not only to the Father, but also to the Son, because Christ was foreshadowed in the Old Law ... In like manner, the New Law corresponds not only to Christ, but also to the Holy Spirit, according

to Romans 8:2: *The law of the Spirit of life in Christ Jesus,* etc. Hence we are not to look forward to another law corresponding to the Holy Spirit.

In other words, the whole Trinity is always present to its creation, is always active in history. To the mission of the Son succeeded that of the Spirit, but that occurred already at Pentecost. Whatever is to come in the future will involve the Son as well.

With respect to the kingdom he simply says in the reply to the fourth objection: "Since Christ said at the very outset of the preaching of the Gospel: *The kingdom of heaven is at hand* (Matt. 4:17), it is most absurd to say that the Gospel of Christ is not the Gospel of the kingdom."

And so with harsh words like *vanitas* and *stultissimum* (most foolish) he rejects the *Eternal Gospel* of Gerard's distorted Joachimism, as well as Joachim's Trinitarian scheme of history.

In a Quodlibetal Question (q. 13, a. 1) on the possibility of a massive defection in the church from the ideal of Gospel poverty, a difficulty is raised that nowadays the church has armies (*castra*) at her disposal. In his reply, based on Augustine, he does admit different temporal *states* of the church but not a fundamental discontinuity.

> Augustine replies in a letter *Against the Donatists,* based on Psalm 2:1: "why do the nations rage?" He distinguishes different times of the Church. There was a time when kings resisted Christ, and at that time they did not give support to the faithful but killed them. But now is another time when kings understand and the learned serve the Lord Jesus Christ in fear, etc., and so in this time kings are vassals of the Church. And so there is another state of the church then and now, but there is not another church.[9]

[9]Thomas Aquinas, *Quaestiones Quodlibetales,* ed. R. Spiazzi (Turin: Marietti, 1956), pp. 231f., no. 244 (19).

This is an indication of considerable social optimism, as well as a high evaluation of the Christian empire, but makes the empire still subordinate to the church.

Finally, dealing with speculations on the millennium, Thomas expresses scepticism about foretelling the future by the concords of the Old and New Testaments:

> I do not think that these persecutions were prophetically signified by those deeds done in Egypt, although by those who think this, individual events from both periods exquisitely and ingeniously seem to be compared: this is done not by a prophetic spirit but by the conjecture of the human mind which sometimes arrives at the truth and sometimes fails. And the same should be said about the sayings of the Abbot Joachim who by such conjectures sometimes predicted truly about future events and in some matters was deceived.

Thomas' critique of Joachim's method of finding harmonies between the Testaments is trenchant and reasonable, but there is an alternative danger of spiritualizing, ahistorical exegesis of a kind dependent on the Pseudo-Denis. Thomas himself is not always immune from this danger, and Albert, as we will see, is even more prey to it. The value of Joachim's method is as a corrective counterweight which takes the events of history with full religious seriousness.[10]

Before turning to Albert, let us summarize some of the factors which inhibited Thomas in his appreciation of a theology of history which is implied in a this-worldly coming of the kingdom and which was represented in his own day in a somewhat deformed way by Joachite speculations and expectations. First of all he probably realized the socially disruptive potential of this theology and, since he had family

[10]Cf. DeLubac's balanced judgment, *Exégèse Médiévale*, vol. 3, p. 556f. Joachim's own contrast of *allegoria* and *concordia*, both of which he accepts, may be found in McGinn, *Apocalyptic*, pp. 122-124, from the *Concordia*, Book 2, Part 1, Chapters 3 and 4.

connections with the Hohenstaufen emperors, was on friend-
ly terms with the saintly French king, Louis IX, and from
time to time served as a theologian at the papal court, he
wanted to help them to maintain the fragile social fabric as it
then was. Secondly, the anti-mendicant controversy and the
excesses of Gerard of Borgo San Donnino threatened the
very existence of the friars. Under these circumstances it
would have been unwise to encourage apocalyptic expectations. Third, Thomas' chief claim to social boldness and
apostolic heroism was his effort to meet the intellectual and
spiritual needs of the new class of urban lay intellectuals and
merchants by the integration of Aristotelian science and
Christian faith. To do this he had to emphasize sober
theological restraint and timeless necessary truths, rather
than the caprice of historical change.[11] Fourth, Thomas'
secular learning is predominantly philosophical rather than
historical and his approach to Scripture and theology is
predominantly sapiential rather than polemical or prophetic
or historical.[12] He also had a strong conviction about the
absolute finality and sole sufficiency of Jesus Christ as well
as about the present work of the Holy Spirit and those were
at least compromised by Joachimism. The great works of
Greek, Roman and Jewish historiography were simply not
available to him, nor were the pseudepigraphical works of
Jewish apocalyptic.[13] Finally, we may note that he did not

[11]Cf. B. Smalley, *The Study of the Bible in the Middle Ages*, 2nd rev. ed.
(Oxford: Blackwell, 1952), p. 292.

[12]But his great tract on prophecy in the *Summa theol.*, II-II, qq. 171-174, con-
tained enough power to ignite a Savonarola. See McGinn, *Apocalyptic*, p. 304, n.
10. On sapiential versus polemical styles in Thomas and Luther, see O.H. Pesch,
"Existential and Sapiential Theology: Luther and Aquinas," in J. Wicks, ed.,
Catholic Scholars Dialogue With Luther (Chicago: Loyola, 1970), pp. 61-81. On
Thomas and Joachim see W.H.J. Schachten, *Ordo Salutis: Das Gesetz als Weise
der Heilsvermittlung. Zur Kritik des hl. Thomas von Aquin an Joachim von Fiore*
(BGPTMA, N.F., 20; Münster: Aschendorff, 1980); Jose Ignatio Saranyana, *Joa-
quin de Fiore y Thomas de Aquino* (Pamplona: Ediciones Universidad de Navarra,
1979).

[13]For a fuller and more balanced presentation of Thomas' relation to history, see
Max Seckler, *Das Heil in der Geschichte. Geschichtstheologisches Denken bei
Thomas von Aquin* (Munich: Kösel, 1964).

complete his great *Summa* so that we do not have his last word on eschatology, but if we judge from the sketch at the end of the *Summa contra Gentiles* this would not have altered the picture significantly.

With Albert (1206-1280) we are in a different world. Although he has much to say about the kingdom, he nowhere, so far as I can see, discusses it in terms of Joachim's theology of history. We are back in the world of Plato, the Pseudo-Denis, and Augustine, but with the addition of Aristotle. We can treat him last because he lived longer than Thomas and Bonaventure, and because his great commentaries on the four canonical gospels[14] were given their final form toward the end of his life, between 1270 and 1276.[15] These commentaries are the only certainly authentic works among the various commentaries on New Testament books attributed to him.[16] They have not yet been critically edited unfortunately. They are masterpieces of medieval university exegesis, always striving for the literal truth, the *veritas litterae*. Perhaps Spicq does not exaggerate when he says that "à ce titre, ... il est le créateur de l'exégèse scientifique."[17] For our purposes we have checked every reference to the kingdom of God in his commentary on the synoptics and found the richest material in his commentary on Matthew, to which he refers back in the rest of his references.

Albert gives a preliminary definition of the kingdom of God at its first occurrence, in Matthew 3:2. His fullest treatment is found when he comes to the Lord's Prayer, at

[14]These four commentaries are found in the Borgnet edition (Paris: Vives, 1893), in volumes 20-24.

[15]Cf. J.M. Vosté, "Sanctus Albertus Magnus Evangeliorum interpres," *Angelicum* 9 (1932): 242-246. Also published in book form, *S. Albertus Magnus sacrae paginae magister* (Rome: Angelico, 1932), vol. 1, pp. 3-62.

[16]C. Spicq, *Esquisse d'une histoire de l'exégèse latine au moyen âge* (Bibliothèque thomiste, 26; Paris: Vrin, 1944), p. 296.

[17]Spicq, *Esquisse*, p. 298. Other treatments of Albert's exegesis may be found in Smalley, *Study*, pp. 298-302 and *passim*, and H. deLubac, *Exégèse médiévale*, vol. 4, pp. 302-307. See also the brief notices in G.G. Meerseman, *Introductio in opera omnia B. Alberti Magni O.P.* (Brugge: Beyaert, 1931), pp. 92-96.

6:10. This runs to eight quarto pages. All the other comments are comparatively brief. Our procedure then will be first to present a translation and analysis of the first definition, then to summarize his shorter, scattered remarks, and then thirdly to concentrate on his full dress treatment. We will conclude with an overall evaluation in light of contemporary theology and exegesis.

> The kingdom of the heavens is threefold: (1) one, which is within us, Luke 17:21: "The Kingdom of God is within you." And this is that concerning which it is said in Romans 14:17: "The Kingdom of God is not eating and drinking, but righteousness, and peace and joy in the Holy Spirit." And through this Kingdom God reigns in us. For this is, as Dionysius says, "distribution of laws, and precepts, and offices, and classes (*gradus*) and goods which pertain to the civilization (*civilitas*) of the saints." And this is the kingdom of God through which God reigns in us. And as the first kingdom is the soul of the true (or: first) king, whose insights (*illuminationes*) and orders and laws and acts as they take effect among the people themselves constitute the kingdom, so this kingdom is first of all in the mind of God, and then, when it is promulgated among the saints, makes up the kingdom of the heavens. And that which in heaven is external to ourselves (*extra nos*) is like to this; but it is even more like the kingdom/reign of the mind of God, which is third, and exemplar, and object, and cause of the two other kingdoms. And it consists in three things: (a) in the enlightening of those who belong to the kingdom, and (b) in the powers of the kingdom, and (c) in the duties actually (*ad actum*) exercised. (2) The second kingdom is the kingdom of the heavens outside of ourselves, which is the place and the honor and the joy (*jucunditas*) of those reigning *in heaven*. And this is acquired by the first kingdom (the one within us). (3) The third kingdom is the one which is the object and cause of these: and this is God descending into both the kingdom within us and the kingdom in heaven. Wisdom 3:8: "They will rule over

peoples, and the Lord will reign over them for ever."
Isaiah 33:22: "The Lord is our king."[18]

Comment: Albert's understanding of the kingdom of God may be summarized as follows: the kingdom consists of three realities, the life of virtues within the soul of the believer, the life of the saints in heaven, and thirdly, God himself. But as Albert understands the third aspect there is really an underlying unity which binds all three aspects together and that is the divine reality present to itself, to the soul and to the blessed. In a word, for Albert the kingdom of God is God himself. This is a relatively original concept in the history of interpretation of this biblical theme. Before Albert the kingdom had been interpreted either as virtue or the resurrection or as the Christian empire or as the church, either the present church or the future church of the Spirit, even as Christ but not, in any major witness, as God. Let us take a closer look at the text to see what might have led Albert to his peculiar view.

His starting point is unpromising enough, because he begins with the least representative text in the Gospels, Luke 17:21: "the kingdom of God is within you." This much abused text has usually misled readers to the conclusion that the kingdom is an inner spiritual reality in the soul of the believer without any future social referent except resurrection to eternal life with the saints in heaven. But if translated as "the kingdom of God is *among* you, i.e., in your midst," and read in context, viz., as addressed to unbelieving Pharisees, as following upon a healing miracle (Luke 17:11-19) and as introducing an entire discourse on *future* eschatology (Luke 17:22-18:8), then the verse yields a view which fits better with the predominantly future sense of the kingdom present throughout Luke and the entire synoptic tradition. The verse would then mean that, while the fullness of the kingdom is yet to come, it is already sufficiently discernible in the

[18]*Albertus Magnus, Enarrationes in Evangelium Matthaei*, 3:2, Borgnet ed. (Paris: Vives, 1893), vol. 20, p. 94.

healing deeds of Jesus to lead eyewitnesses to a decision of faith in Jesus as the divinely accredited agent of the kingdom. It has nothing to do with a kind of private, individualistic pietism.[19] But all of this was not apparent to Albert, who depended upon the Vulgate's *intra vos* (within you).

After this false start, Albert unwittingly veers toward the best and truest definition of the kingdom to be found in the New Testament: Romans 14:17: "the kingdom of God is not in food and drink but justice and peace and joy in the Holy Spirit." Had he understood these values as a promise for an earthly future and as social goods he would have been quite correct. But his understanding of these realities is dominated by his privatized view of the kingdom which he derived from Luke 17:21, so he takes them to be purely inner magnitudes, and thereby strips them of their innate social, transformative power. For Albert God reigns in our hearts but not directly in the world. (Perhaps such a low view of God's power to influence and to direct the turn of historical events may be attributed to Albert's depressing episcopal experiences at close range with the workings of the Christian church and empire, and especially to his bitter experiences at having preached the crusade (ca. 1263) which went down to defeat at the Horns of Hattin (1187) and finally lost even the miserable little toehold of St. Jean d'Acre (1291). With the fall of Acre went an archbishopric and a Dominican province.)

Perhaps this line of interpretation which we have been pursuing is misdirected. Perhaps Albert is not so unsocial after all. A judgment in this matter depends in part on our interpretation of the next sentences in which Albert is drawing upon a phrase of the Pseudo-Denis: "[The kingdom

---

[19]Augustin Georges, *Etudes sur l'oeuvre de Luc* (Paris: Gabalda, 1978), pp. 297-298. When Albert himself comes to comment on this verse, he will recognize this. After discussing other meanings, he then concludes: "Nevertheless according to the letter here [Jesus] means that a material kingdom is already present *among* the Pharisees: because the king of the righteous, and the first ordering of powers, and of the princes of the Apostles and disciples was *in their midst*, and they did not recognize him."

of God is] the distribution of laws, and precepts, and offices and classes (*gradus*) and goods which pertain to the civilization of the saints."[20]

From his comments on this passage it appears that Albert is not an unpolitical theologian. Rather he works out of the Platonic mode of political theory which is psychologizing and idealistic. For Plato the ideal ruler is a philosopher, and his principal means of directing his citizens is educational and rhetorical, winning their hearts and minds through persuasion. The Christian neo-Platonism of the Pseudo-Denis which Albert follows transports this model of political theory into the mind of God. It too is concerned with laws, offices, social classes and civilization in general. For Albert the divine mind works through persuasion, order, and actions. Thus there is an unmistakably social dimension to this thought. Albert thinks of the kingdom as the divine rule, not in specifically territorial terms. This is possible for him because the Latin term in question, *regnum*, can mean both *kingdom*, in the sense of a territory under royal government, and the actual governing activity, *rule* (*Herrschaft*). This interpretation is supported by much contemporary biblical scholarship which prefers to translate *basileia toû theoû* as rule or reign of God. This translation however fails to catch the earthly, territorial reference of the biblical concept, so that many exegetes, the present writer included, still prefer the translation "kingdom".[21] But there can be no doubt that Albert is catching an aspect of the biblical meaning. And as Plato's *Republic* can be interpreted both psychologically and politically, so for Albert God's rule of hearts is also a rule of the state and sovereignty called the kingdom of God.

Concluding our analysis of this key passage we note simply that for Albert the second phase of the kingdom is

[20]So far as I can tell, this is a loose quotation from Dionysius the Areopagite's treatise *On the Divine Names,* ch. 12 (PG 3, 969 A; *Dionysiaca,* I, p. 527; the translation into Latin is that of John Sarracenus).

[21]S. Aalen, "Reign and House in the Kingdom of God in the Gospels," *New Testament Studies* 8 (1961-2) 215-240.

the heaven of the saints, and that the third, which holds the other two together, is God himself. What is most striking in all of this is Albert's Platonic way of grasping and failing to grasp the social dimension of the biblical concept.

Turning now to the second part of our study of Albert, we will simply present without comment some of his more striking and original remarks on the kingdom. On Matthew 6:33, noting that Chrysostom says that the kingdom of God is here eternal retribution, Albert comments: 'This is true with respect to the ultimate goal intended. But the kingdom which we are here enjoined to seek is that by which God reigns among men. The meaning is "First," by struggling, preaching, working well (*militando, praedicando, bene operando*), constantly "seek the kingdom of God," i.e., that he reign by a strengthened kingdom-rule over men. "And its righteousness," i.e., the justice by which this reign is strengthened, and which leads to an everlasting reign.'

On Matthew 13:31 he observes: "The kingdom of heaven is not like the kingdoms of other powers. For these rule by coercive force (*virtute coactiva*). But the heavenly kingdoms attract us by the force of love (*virtute ... amativa*)." Commenting on Matthew 25:1, the parable of the wise and foolish virgins, he says: "The kingdom of heaven is here understood as the pursuit of beauty which is set before man according to the laws which lead to heaven." On Luke 17:21a he teaches the *universality* of the kingdom which he contrasts with the provincialism of the Donatists in Africa and of the Arians elsewhere: "regnum enim gratiae Dei, in potestate saeculari non erit: neque in una parte mundi, sed in toto mundo, quia totum orbem obtinebit" (For the kingdom of the grace of God will not consist in worldly power; nor will it be in only one part of the world, but in the whole world, because it will inherit the entire globe).

Finally we come to Albert's fullest treatment of the theme, his commentary on the phrase of the Lord's Prayer, *Adveniat Regnum Tuum, Thy Kingdom Come.*[22] His extensive obser-

---

[22]Borgnet ed. vol. 20, pp. 265-272.

vations fall into three parts. (1) What is a *kingdom*, and what is this kingdom? (2) In what way is this kingdom the kingdom of *God the Father*? (3) Why do we pray that it *come*? thus each of the terms *Regnum Tuum Adveniat* is analyzed separately. Of these three sections the longest giving the definition of the kingdom, is the first. It contains a remarkable compendium of political philosophy, drawing upon Plato, *Democratica* (?), *Timaeus*, Aristotle, *Ethics*, *Politics*, and *De Regimine Dominorum* (?), Cicero, *Rhetorica prima*, Ambrose, Augustine, and the Pseudo-Denis. In this section Albert first attempts a definition and characterization of a kingdom or state in general and then (pp. 269-271) applies these data to the religious concept of the kingdom of God. At a high point in the discussion of the second section, Albert spontaneously bursts into a prayer (pp. 272). The third, brief section represents a sound and balanced theology of grace in which God's initiative is primary, but includes and invites our human, free response.

Leaning on Plato, Albert defines a kingdom as:

> nothing other than complete power and dominion in a single person, animate justice, ordered by laws, concretized by urban communities as its parts, strengthened by the force of arms, governing according to the best principles of civilization, superabounding in external goods and supplied with sufficient organic resources ... And if this power were not in a single person, but were a divided power, then division and schism could arise, and thence desolation ... A body with many heads is a monstrous thing.

Albert then proceeds further to define each element in this definition and his definitions are amplified and supported both by classical and patristic authors and by frequent quotations from the Bible, particularly from the historical books of the Old Testament, as well as from the prophets and wisdom literature. This section is characterized by practical common sense, as well as by some bizarre military ideas derived from the *Timaeus*, but the whole discussion is conducted in terms of classical antiquity with no reference to specifically contemporary events or conditions, although, when Albert reports a class of unmarried soldiers in Plato's ideal scheme, he might be thinking of the military religious orders of his own day. His definition of justice is the standard Aristotelian *suum cuique tribuere* (to give to each his own), rather than the more Christian definition of Augustine and Peter Lombard: *iustitia est in subveniendis miseris* (justice consists in helping the needy).

Albert then turns his attention to how all this applies to the kingdom of God. His approach is highly spiritual and moral.

> Taking all these matters into our spiritual lives (*in spiritualibus*), then the divine processions [of the Trinity] create the dominion of the kingdom in us, elevating, enriching and strengthening us. These processions are rays of divine grace, which lift the heart up from anything which would depress it into servitude, so that now we should disdain to look at such things, but be powerfully lifted beyond them, and crush them, and be filled with beautiful and good things as by a fountain (*fontaliter*). By this means we are sublimated above the vile (*vilia*) and never fall into them.

Albert then takes most of the elements of the Platonic definition and interprets them in terms of the spiritual life of the believer. Thus "justice must be our everlasting life." "the divine laws are engraved on our hearts to be kept inviolably." Urban structures are interpreted as the duties of the virtues. The seven women who embrace one man in Isaiah 4:1 become the seven virtues (theological and cardinal). The weapons in this kingdom are "studies, alertness and Scripture, by which the enemy devil is kept out." We also share in the legions of the angelic hosts, grouped in the nine choirs of the Pseudo-Denis. And so on.

> Thus God the Father confirms his kingdom in us, by giving us a share in his lordship through grace, by which he raises us up and assimilates us to his Son the king, who sits at his right hand. Colossians 3:1f.

In the second section Albert explains why this kingdom belongs to the Father. "In it he reigns, he gives it to the Son, through the Son he leads believers to adoptive sonship, and at the end of time the kingdom will be turned over to him by the Son with all who are in it and it in them." Each of these four aspects is then supported by Scripture quotations. The most dynamically eschatological among these four aspects is the last, which looks forward to a definitive divine resolution of history, based on I Corinthians 15:24: "then comes the end, when he delivers the kingdom to God the Father after destroying every rule and every authority and power." This verse presupposes a Jewish apocalyptic world view for its full understanding, but Albert did not have such a world view at his disposal and the implications of the verse remain undeveloped in his commentary.

When Albert turns to the third and final term in the clause *Thy Kingdom come, Adveniat*, his commentary becomes a little treatise on the theology of grace, in which the accent falls on the primacy of the divine initiative and yet we are called to a response. Thus he stands in the same line as Augustine and Thomas.

> It does not say that we should come to the kingdom [but that the kingdom come to us]. This is because we do not of ourselves have the power to do so. But if it should first come to us, then we can finally *by its force* come to it. ...
> Since the kingdom of God is the power of perfect right-eousness, the kingdom comes to us when it goes ahead of us (*nos praeveniens*) and lays claim to us [and liberates us, *vindicat sibi*], and then associates us in a common work, that we might cooperate with it toward the establishment of the kingdom ... No one arrives at the honor of the

kingdom, until the kingdom has first come to him
through the keeping of the laws and virtues and righteousness and power in the aforesaid manner. (p. 272).

It is time for a concluding evaluation of Albert's teaching
on the kingdom. This may be quickly accomplished by two
observations, one laudatory, one carping. Albert passes the
test of Tillich's four-point definition of the kingdom: it is
political, social, personalistic and universal. But for Albert
the kingdom of God is only political in the Platonic
psychologico-political sense. In general we may speak of an
emphatic spiritualizing tendency in Albert's thought on this
point, which makes his doctrine unsuitable as a theological
basis for radical social doctrines today. This is confirmed by
our second observation. Albert fails the test of comprehend-
ing the Jewish this-wordly inner-historical eschatological
divine intervention which was the specific content of Jesus'
own preaching.

In summary, the theology of the Middle Ages did not well
understand the this-worldly future dimension of the kingdom of God. We have seen this to be the case in the great
theologians of high scholasticism, Bonaventure, Thomas
Aquinas, and Albert of Cologne. The challenge of the kingdom was mediated to Bonaventure and Thomas primarily
by the three state theology of history of Joachim of Flora.
This theology implied that the dispensation under Christ was
not final but that a third dispensation, under the Holy Spirit,
was still to come before the end of the world. Bonaventure
responded with partial sympathy, Thomas with sharp dis-
missal. Albert pursued his own path, apparently unaffected
by Joachism. His path was one of Platonizing Christian
spirituality which identified the kingdom with God himself.
The failure of medieval theology to integrate a this-worldly
eschatology is one of its major weaknesses, yet the influence
of Joachite hopes continued underground until well into the
modern period.

Appendix to Chapter 3

The Kingdom of God in Meister Eckhart and John of Paris

After the great theological syntheses of the thirteenth century, the late Middle Ages of the fourteenth and early fifteenth centuries entered into an agonizing transition to the modern world, troubled by plague and crusader failure, schism between church and state, between church and church, pope and pope, pope and council, nation-state and nation-state, faith and reason. In the midst of these troubles, there was progress in art and architecture, communication and trade, science and technology. Chaucer reflects a rather secure and stable world, pulsing with humor and vitality as well as knightly and religious idealism. Religious interest remained high, especially when a preacher could present the Christian truths in a fresh way, in vernacular speech and paradoxical imagery. Meister Eckhart was the right man for those times.

Born near Erfurt in Saxony around 1260, Eckhart rose quickly in the Dominican order as master of theology, prior and provincial, till he was accused of error by the archbishop of Cologne. He appealed to the Pope in Avignon but died in 1327, before twenty-eight of his propostions were condemned. A scholastic mystic who existentialized Albert and Thomas, Eckhart treats of the kingdom chiefly in two works: a sermon on Luke 21:31, and a treatise on the Lord's Prayer. In the sermon,[1] Eckhart follows his predecessor Albert when he says: "The kingdom of God is God himself with all his wealth." He goes on to make the point that when the Scriptures say that the kingdom is near this means that

[1] *Breakthrough: Meister Eckhart's Creation Spirituality In New Translation*, ed. Matthew Fox (New York: Doubleday-Image, 1980, pp. 137-141. (Sermon 9 in the Fox edition equals sermon 36 in Quint's German edition and sermon 6 in the Blakney translation.)

God is near to all who call upon him with a sincere heart, always and everywhere, because he is beyond space and time.

In the treatise on the Lord's Prayer Eckhart says that "we are heaven ... if we want our Father to be in us." "Thy Kingdom come" means first that "by the extinction of our vices, God might reign in us or rather in the whole world through the abundance of virtue. Second, the prayer refers to the future kingdom of which Jesus spoke."[2] The prayer then bids "this very earth to become a heaven." If these insights could be put together (earthly and future), then Eckhart would have recaptured Jesus' own eschatology. Fox speaks of Eckhart's "realized eschatology"[3] but he means by this Eckhart's desire for a future realization of God's promises here on earth rather than what Dodd means, viz., that through the gift of the Spirit the promises have already been realized (see chapter 5). Finally, in his little treatise on the true aristocrat,[4] Eckhart provides a mystical basis for egalitarian democracy. "Who then is more royal than one who was born, on the one hand, from the highest and best that a creature possesses and, on the other hand, from the most intimate depths of the divine nature and its wilderness?"[5] Eckhart remains to the end an intellectual contemplative, yet the boldness of his language and imagery contributed to the loosening of feudal ties.[6]

[2]Fox, pp. 495-503.

[3]Pp. 44f.

[4]Fox, pp. 510-518; Blakney, pp. 74-81.

[5]Fox develops the implications here further in "Meister Eckhart and Karl Marx: The Mystic as Political Theologian," *Listening* 13 (1978) 233-257, reprinted in Richard Woods, ed., *Understanding Mysticism* (New York: Doubleday-Image, 1980), pp. 541-563.

[6]While Eckhart was being condemned under Pope John XXII, so were the Franciscan Spirituals. At the same time, a controversy about beatitude as the beatific vision raged around this pope. The practical outcome was the loss of the Jewish apocalyptic social dimension as a description of salvation, in favor of Hellenistic immortalitism. Walter Ong has proposed that we replace beatific vision terminology with language about the divine *presence* which is English for the biblical Greek *parousia*, the divine *arrival*. Cf. Ong, *The Presence of the Word* (New Haven: Yale, 1967).

Another type of late medieval reflection which contributed to the rise of the secular state is the theological-canonical treatise on royal and papal power. A good example is a work of that name by John of Paris (Jean Quidort, O.P.).[7] John wrote his treatise around 1302/3 as an effort to mediate in the dispute between Pope Boniface VIII and King Philip the Fair of France. In his Proemium, John of Paris sets as his main objective the discovery of the truth about priestly power in temporal affairs. He is obviously trying to mediate between Eusebian and Augustinian views (as we have outlined them in our second chapter), after they have come into collision due to an extreme papalist development of Augustine's teaching that the kingdom on earth is to be found in the church. John compares the extreme papalists to king Herod.

> who on learning of the birth of a king called Christ believed that his kingship was of the human kind. Certain moderns seem to have taken their views from this source. For they have moved so far from the first error as to assert that the pope, in so far as he stands in Christ's place on earth has a power over the properties of princes and barons as well as cognizance and jurisdiction of them. They say that the pope has power in temporalities in a more excellent way than the prince because he has primary authority, derived directly from God, whereas the prince has his power mediately from God through the pope.[8]

In his eighth chapter John denies that any direct papal jurisdiction over other's property could be derivable from Christ since Christ himself had no such jurisdiction even though he was king twice over, as creator, and as God made

---

[7]There are two recent translations, one by J.A. Watt (Toronto: Pontifical Institute of Medieval Studies, 1971), one by A.P. Monahan (New York: Columbia University, 1974). We will refer to Watt.

[8]*Proemium*, p. 71.

man. John denies that Christ was king simply as man and invokes his poor and simple life style as proof. He cites Eusebius [tainted source!] in support and refers the Daniel prophecy (7:14) to heaven alone, even though Daniel and Revelation make clear that the kingdom of the Son of Man, the new Jerusalem, comes to earth: "And to him was given dominion and glory and kingdom ... his kingdom [is] one that shall not be destroyed." "And I saw the holy city, new Jerusalem, coming down out of heaven from God" (Rev 21:2).

4. THE KINGDOM OF GOD IN THE EARLY MODERN PERIOD

As we leave the Middle Ages and move into the Renaissance and Reformation, Baroque, Enlightenment and Romantic eras, it can be easy for us to lose our path. On the one hand, there is a flood of interesting, somewhat relevant, figures and movements in this long period. On the other hand, our narrow theme of the apocalyptic kingdom of God as preached by Jesus is not the center of ecclesiastical life or thought in this period, with marginal exceptions, until the end of the eighteenth century. Even this bland assertion could be endlessly qualified. We will proceed by brief notices of most figures until we come to the hero of the story in this period, Immanual Kant. Such a choice of hero is in many respects surprising, and could be misleading. The present writer is not in most respects a Kantian. But even a philosopher with whom one has one's differences can be acknowledged to have had some insights into truth, some at least partially beneficent influences. Nor do we intend to suggest that Kant's interpretation of the kingdom of God is in every respect adequate from the viewpoint of modern historical exegesis. It is not. What we do claim is that Kant's positive concentration on this religious theme in the work of his old age brought the kingdom of God to the center of theological attention and shifted high-cultural interest away from other themes to this one. Since Kant it has only left the center stage for brief intervals, while today it conquers more and more intellectual provinces.

I. Renaissance and Reformation

The Renaissance was, among other things, a revival of
classical antiquity. Aided by printing, early pagan and Christian texts were collected and studied. It became fashionable
to learn Greek but Hebrew too had its devotees. The shift
away from philosophy to rhetoric, esthetics and philology
aided the historical comprehension of ancient texts. The
Renaissance is a complex phenomenon, with Italian and
Northern European, pagan and Christian components.
Within the Renaissance there were elements which could
assist in the gradual rediscovery of the Jewish-Christian
theme of an apocalyptic kingdom of God. But there were
enough elements moving in the opposite direction to prevent
the Renaissance from retrieving the concept in its fullness.
Helpful elements were the interest in philology, Greek studies, history, especially Ximenes' and Erasmus' editions of
the Greek New Testament (1514, 1515 respectively) and
Santes Pagnini's guide to the Hebrew Bible. To Erasmus
also falls the honor of publishing Irenaeus for the first time
(1526). Recovery and publication of Jewish apocalyptic
pseudepigrapha would only flourish in the Baroque and
modern periods but the appetite for Jewish exotica began
with Pico della Mirandola's interest in the works of cabbalis-
tic mysticism. Obstacles to understanding the kingdom were,
it seems, the renewed interest in neoplatonism and the neopagan hostility to biblical faith.

It is our judgment that the bold synthesis of Aristotelian
science and Christian faith achieved by Thomas Aquinas
kept the rising class of lay intellectuals largely within the
church from say 1250 to 1450. From then on the synthesis
fell apart or was much more difficult to maintain. The
greatest religious figure of the Italian renaissance, Jerome
Savonarola (1452-1498), derived his own powerful reforming
inspiration not only from the Bible but from prophetic
impulses of the Joachite movement and, even more explicitly,
from the treatise on prophecy in Aquinas' *Summa theologiae*,
II-II, qq. 171-178, the work of his Dominican confrere. He
was sufficiently inspired to move the people of Florence by

his preaching to overthrow the ruling Medici family and to declare their city-state a republic of which Christ alone was king. That decree has never been formally rescinded. His preaching contained useful criticisms of evils in clergy, papacy and society but he was drawn into unwise predictions of historical events and some of his practical proposals, such as burning art works which savored too much of a pagan spirit, have been viewed by art lovers at least as socially regressive, an attempt to return to the Middle Ages. Thus our final judgment on him must remain uncertain. But that he kept the prophetic critique of society alive and looked to God's intervention in history (through Charles VIII of France) to restore Christendom, that he strove for a theocratic democracy - these cannot be doubted. If he did not plan for the kingdom of God, he did build a republic of Christ.

Shortly before Savonarola was hanged as a heretic in a public square of Florence, Christopher Columbus had discovered a new world across the Atlantic. His quest had been partly inspired by Joachite aspirations and gave rise in its turn to utopian thoughts and missionary projects. The Jesuit "reductions" in Paraguay were a kind of utopian community for baptized Indians, paternalistically progressive. Their great man in Brazil, Antonio Vieira (1608-1697), worked tirelessly for the improvement of the conditions of the Indians, his preaching filled with prophetic inspiration. He ended his days in Bahia, working on his *Key to the Prophets*, an unfinished work devoted to the consummation of Christ's kingdom on earth. After the suppression of the Jesuits in 1773 their Joachite missionary inspiration passed to the Franciscans, especially to Junipero Serra, who built twenty missions along the California coast, each with a utopian-restrictive plan for the improvement of Indian life.

The new world inspired not only missionary zeal but also provided men of thought to devise schemes of ideal societies. Among the first of these in our period was St. Thomas More's *Utopia* (1516). In it he describes an ideal community living according to the natural law and practicing a natural religion, with many satiric side-thrusts at contemporary abuses. Indeed, his playful spirit makes his work less relevant to our concern than another utopian thinker, Tommaso Campanella (1568-1639). A Dominican friar whose political interests caused him to spend much of his adult life in prison and to be tortured seven times (he was suspected of plotting to overthrow Spanish rule in the kingdom of Naples), he composed while imprisoned a significant little work, *The City of the Sun* (1623). His own utopia showed influences from the description of the Inca kingdom in Peru as well as from Plato's *Republic*, Augustine and Thomas. He envisaged a society tightly structured in concentric circles involving a static class system and even a plurality of wives (this last a Platonic touch). The whole was to be under the control of philosopher-priests who would submit the government of the state to the supreme authority of the Pope. Most disappointing from a religious point of view is that the religious dimension is reduced to natural law and the sacraments. From a political science viewpoint what is distressing is the bureaucratic centralization, the "pathos of order," with no room for play or for the accidental. Less fluid as a thinker than his great antecedent Giordano Bruno, Campanella constructed a static cathedral of social order. He is the sort of man who gives utopias a bad name. Yet without imagining possible better futures, no better futures are possible.[1]

As a powerful return to the Scriptures, the Reformation should have meant a rediscovery of the biblical message of the kingdom. In fact, this is not true of the mainstream of the Protestant Reformation, Lutheran, Calvinist, and Angli-

[1] I am persuaded by Ernst Bloch's *Vorlesungen zur Philosophie der Renaissance* (Frankfurt A.M.: Suhrkamp, 1972) that the serious philosophy of the Renaissance is to be found in Bruno and Campanella, not in the rhetorical figures like Pico and Ficino. A conservative critique of all utopian thinking is to be found in Thomas Molnar's *Utopia, The Perennial Heresy* (New York: Sheed & Ward, 1967). A more sympathetic view can be found in F.E. and F.P. Manuel, *Utopian Thought in the Western World.* (Cambridge, MA: Harvard-Belknap, 1980). There is also a useful review article by Harry Levin on the Manuels' book which provides some correctives, in *New York Review* (6 March 1980) 47-50. Peter Shaffer's *Royal Hunt of the Sun* (1964) dramatizes the tension between totalitarian utopia and anarchic, even unjust, freedom in terms of the Incas and Pizarro's *conquistadores*.

can, but only of more marginal groups like the Anabaptists, and later, the Pietists. The main reason for this is that the classical Reformation was primarily concerned with a radicalization of the Pauline-Augustinian message of salvation by grace through faith alone. To this the Calvinists added an interest in the Hebrew Scriptures and the Anglicans eventually a predilection for the Fourth Gospel. But the main focus was not on the synoptic gospels, except for the Lucan parables about the forgiveness of sins.

That is the broad picture as we see it, but of course there are qualifications and nuances. Let us begin with Martin Luther. We take it for granted that Luther was a religious genius of gigantic proportions, whose heritage is quite complex and mixed. Incontrovertibly positive in their effects were his vernacular preaching, catechisms, hymns and Bible translations, his effect on the development of the German language, his attempt to harness the humanist Renaissance to the service of the Scriptures, his reform of theology through a return to its sources, his pastoral zeal, above all his personal religious seriousness. The social, political and ecclesial effects of his reform are more variously evaluated. There are also some surprising twists. For example, Burckhardt and Bainton have concluded that, due to his criticism and partly contrary to his intention, Luther saved the papacy as a religious institution from disintegrating into a petty Italian city state.[2]

Luther is such an enormous figure it is hard to know where to begin with him. We will proceed from his theory to the practical effects of his teaching, and, within the theory, from the more formal public statements of policy to more occasional utterances.

We begin with a classic statement of the Lutheran position, the Augsburg Confession, presented to the emperor Charles V in 1530. This statement was not written by Luther himself, but by his humanist colleague Philip Melanchthon.

---

[2]Jacob Burckhardt, *The Civilization of the Renaissance in Italy* (London: Phaidon, 1950; orig. ed. 1860), p. 76-79; Roland Bainton, *Erasmus of Rotterdam* (New York: Scribner, 1969), last chapter.

Melanchthon then followed this up with an Apology (1531) which is even more explicit. The relevant articles are 16 on civil government, and 17 on the return of Christ for judgment. The former teaches full submission to the state in all save sin, and goes on to say that "the Gospel does not teach an outward and temporal but an inward and eternal mode of existence and righteousness of the heart." The latter, while admitting a return of the Lord for judgment and resurrection, rejects "certain Jewish opinions which are even now making an appearance and which teach that, before the resurrection of the dead, saints and godly men will possess a worldly kingdom and annihilate all the godless."

To understand these sentences a few comments are in order. First, when the text speaks of Gospel, this does not mean the four written gospels, Matthew, Mark, Luke, and John, but Luther's doctrine of justification by faith alone (which he believed to be the central message of Paul and John - much of the rest of the New Testament could be discarded as "Jewish opinions"). Next, because of the preference for an "inward and eternal" righteousness, some commentators have spoken of a residue of mysticism in Lutheranism, and of its "quietism." Of course Christian faith should have an inner basis and a link with eternal life, but as an incarnational and sacramental faith it also has an outward and temporal manifestation in common worship and Christian life. (The Confession goes on to make this point, more clearly in the German than in the Latin text.) Third, it is the contention of our first chapter that the "rejected Jewish opinion" was proclaimed by the Jew Jesus with this qualification, that the kingdom which the godly will possess is the kingdom of God in this world, which brings justice and peace in its train. (The fate of the ungodly is not stressed.)

Melanchton's Apology notes that the Imperial Catholic Confutation (not dogmatic teaching) accepts their article 17 - sad but true, and typical of all mainline churches. The same is true for article 16, but here Melanchthon goes on to clarify the "distinction between Christ's kingdom and a political kingdom. Christ's kingdom is spiritual; it is the knowledge of God in the heart, the fear of God and faith, the beginning of eternal righteousness and eternal life ... The Gospel does not introduce any new laws about the civil estate." He goes on to speak about the "Jewish dream of the messianic kingdom." It is obvious that this approach is virtually identical with the spiritual-mystical interpretation we have already seen in Origen and the neoplatonic tradition as a whole.[3]

What of Luther himself? Because of his vast output, Luther scholars distinguish between his early, his reforming and his later works. Some go so far as to pinpoint the three major treatises of 1520 as the absolutely normative perfection of Luther, as his "primary works." Let us follow this line for simplicity's sake. Here, along with a long essay on the sacraments and the beautiful *Freedom of a Christian*, we find Luther's *Open Letter to the Christian Nobility of the German Nation Concerning the Reform of the Christian Estate*. Here Luther is speaking as a German nationalist, appealing to the emperor Charles V and to the German territorial princes and knights to, in effect, take control of the church for the good of the empire. The work is divided into three parts: I. The three walls of the Romanists are that the spiritual power is above the temporal, that the interpretation of the Scriptures belongs to no one except the pope, that no one can call a council but the pope. II. Abuses to be discussed in councils are the worldly splendor of the pope, the cardinals, and the Roman curia, especially the traffic in benefices, abbacies *in commendam* and dispensations from the incompatibility of offices. (Abbacies held *in commendam* were titles and revenues held by laymen or secular clerics who did not live the monastic life or reside in the abbey.) III. There follow twenty-seven proposals for reform, most having to do with the church. These tend to restrict the authority of the pope, but also include denunciations of pilgrimages, mendicant orders of friars, anniversary masses for the dead, frequent festivals, and begging. There is a strong

[3]Cf. *Die Bekenntnisschriften der evangelisch-lutherischen Kirche* (Göttingen: Vandenhoeck & Ruprecht, 1952), ed. Hans Lietzmann et al, pp. 70-72 and 307-310, and *The Book of Concord*, ed. T.G. Tappert (Philadelphia: Fortress, 1959) pp. 37-39 and 222-224.

encouragement for the marriage of priests. The institution of religious sisterhoods is denounced but no specific charges are brought. Then, at the end, Luther teaches that the Holy Roman Empire of the German Nation should be superior to the pope in temporal matters but that there are five failings of the temporal estate: excess in dress, e.g., the wearing of silk and velvet; excess in eating and drinking; the spice trade should be reduced and commerce restricted; there should be no more annuities, or lending at interest; prostitution should be abolished. The important point for us to note in all this is Luther's tendency to make the emperor and the princes superior to the pope not only in temporal matters but also in spiritual affairs, especially the reform of the church, the convoking of church councils and the like. Thus in practice Luther tended to return to a Constantinian-Carolingian-Ottonian position where the emperor controlled the church, and tried to undo the results of the investiture controversy. But he did this without claiming that the empire was the kingdom of God on earth or that the emperor was the Son of Man. Perhaps Luther's restraint in this regard is due to the emperor's refusal to accept the Augsburg Confesson. But Charles V did sack Rome with the aid of Lutheran troops and he did pressure the pope to convoke the council of Trent.[4]

A third classical element of Luther's teaching relevant to our theme is his doctrine of the two kingdoms.[5] Originating in a concrete problem, the distribution of Bibles in the territory of a prince-bishop, it became one of Luther's basic keys for interpreting and applying the Christian faith to his time. Three years after his *Address to the German Nobility*, Luther wrote 'On Secular Authority, And How Far One Owes Obedience To It'. There he said:

> Here we must divide the children of Adam and all men into two parts, the first belonging to the kingdom of God,

[4]Martin Luther, *Three Treatises* (Philadelphia: Fortress, 1960). pp. 3-111.

[5]See Heinrich Bornkamm, *Luther's Doctrine of the Two Kingdoms* (Philadelphia: Fortress, 1966), and Gerhard Ebeling, *Luther* (London: Collins-Fontana, 1972), pp. 175-191.

and the second to the kingdom of the world. Those who belong to the kingdom of God are all true believers in Christ, and are subject to Christ. For Christ is the King and Lord in the kingdom of God ... The gospel should also be called a gospel of the kingdom of God, because it teaches, governs and maintains the kingdom of God ... All who are not Christians belong to the kingdom of the world and are subject to the law.[6]

Several things are obvious at once. Luther is here influenced by St. Augustine's views in *The City of God*. But Luther was unwilling to identify the kingdom of God with the church on earth, since, unlike earlier Saxon religious leaders (I think of Meister Eckhart), he preferred to turn most of his critical fire on the church itself rather than on the state. Second, it is notorious among specialists that this is a difficult doctrine to grasp in its full complexity. It has sometimes been interpreted as foreshadowing the American separation of church and state, although it is not clear that Luther had this in mind. It has also been understood negatively as a schizoid separation of Christ and culture, of private conscience and the public morality of the state which includes necessarily compromises with evil as well as violence and brutality. Ultimately it cannot be rightly understood without seeing it as a function of an even more basic theological theme of Luther's, the distinction between law and gospel, but that would take us too far from our topic. It must suffice to say that Luther took over Augustinian ideas, radicalized the opposition between the two kingdoms, and then related them paradoxically in the conscience of the individual Christian. For Luther, Christ and culture *are* related but only through paradox. This makes it hard to pin Luther down theoretically. It is therefore all the more important to see how he confronted some concrete issues.

First then he had to relate his movement to the princes. After his appeal to pope, bishop and emperor failed, he was excommunicated and became an outlaw. He accepted protection from the elector of Saxony whose territory he never left thereafter. In his lifetime one other electorate was won over to his cause, Brandenburg, besides various landgravates, duchies, principalities and free cities. As the need to organize territorial churches increased, Luther accepted in practice the leadership and backing of the princes, following the Constantinian model but on a smaller scale. This developed into the institution of the *Summepiscopat*, the territorial prince as the chief bishop or highest officer in and over the church. Things became even more complicated after Luther's death, when one elector became Calvinist and one Catholic. Luther himself was never quite satisfied with this arrangement, developed at times a more spiritual-mystical ecclesiology, and at times could be sharply critical of the nobility. Nevertheless, faced with a choice between prince and pope, he chose the prince and has ever after had to pay the price of being described as a lackey of the princes. This accusation becomes most acute in the case of the Peasants' Revolt.[7]

The Peasants' War was a confused series of uprisings beginning in Swabia, in the south, and spread quickly to other parts of Germany till it affected about a third of the country. It ran through 1524 and 1525, and was brutally put down by Lutheran and Catholic lords alike. It cost the Lutheran movement the support of many peasants and the poor and also aroused the distrust of some princes. We will consider its theological links with the Anabaptists further on. Here we need only note Luther's response. This came in several stages. In their twelve Articles, the peasants not only appealed to a broad range of Scripture, especially Exodus, but they also asked reform theologians, including Luther, for guidance. Luther first replied in a rather balanced way,

[7]See Irmgard Hoss, "The Lutheran Church of the Reformation: Problems of its Formation and Organization in the Middle and North German Territories" in L.P. Buck & J.W. Zophy, *The Social History of the Reformation* (Columbus: Ohio Univ. Press, 1972), pp. 317-339; and A.L. Drummond, *German Protestantism Since Luther* (London: Epworth, 1951) for the subsequent working out of the Reformation in German lands; L. Bouyer, *The Church of God* (Chicago: Franciscan Herald, 1982), pp. 47-54, for Luther's conflicting ecclesiologies.

admonishing both lords and peasants to do their duty, but opposing any kind of rebellion and theologically distinguishing the Gospel (in his sense) from any kind of social program, the kingdom of God from any kind of earthly kingdom. This was his *Admonition to Peace* of 1525. After he was hissed by an angry crowd and had seen the riots in Thuringia, he wrote his famous pamphlet *Against the Robbing and Murdering Hordes of Peasants* (1525). In this he declares the revolt to be the work of the devil and encourages the princes to put the rebels to the sword as though they were mad dogs. Little did he know that this was what they were doing even as he wrote. His work came out after the event and hurt his good name. But he did not retract his remarks. He defended them later in that year in an *Open Letter on the Harsh Book Against the Peasants.*[8]

In assessing Luther's role we note that he was more an artist than a politician, more a church reformer than a social one. He liked social order and was quick to see signs of the end time in any disturbance. In this sense he was highly eschatological. In his use of Scripture on social problems he relies almost exclusively on Romans 13:1-7 which enjoins submission to the state. Unlike a later Lutheran, Oscar Cullmann, Luther did not see that Scripture balances this text with Revelation 13 which describes the state grown demonic. To such a state the Christian owes little but resistance.[9]

Overall assessments of Luther's social teaching and its effects vary considerably, from Ernst Troeltsch's view of its harmful reactionary conservatism and his judgment of its "ethical sterility" to Karl Holl's more positive evaluation. Luther unquestionably pioneered a public school system and improved the quality of marriage and family life. The

[8]The text of Luther's three relevant treatises, together with the Peasants' Twelve Articles are in *Luther's Works*, vol. 46 (Philadelphia: Fortress, 1967). A brief guide to the problem and the literature is Hubert Kirchner's *Luther and the Peasants' War* (Philadelphia: Fortress, 1972). The most famous Marxist criticism is F. Engles, *The Peasant War in Germany.* He was followed by Karl Kautsky and the leaders of the present regime in East Germany. These have recently softened their repudiation of Luther for tourism's sake, but only slightly.

[9]Cullmann, *The State in the New Testament* (New York: Scribner, 1956).

general tendency of his social thinking was conservative. Certainly he was no friend to social or economic revolution. He thought urgently of the endtimes and yet envisaged no divine intervention to rectify things on earth. (He never wrote a commentary on a synoptic gospel. This exegetical choice already suggests his avoidance of Jesuanic eschatology.) The Lutheran heritage is just as confusing. Of the original Lutheran electorate, Saxony, the eastern industrial part became in the twentieth century solidly socialist, "Red Saxony," and forms the mainstay of the East German Communist party. The wooded western part, Thuringia, went solidly Nazi early. Conservative Lutheran theologians like Althaus accepted Hitler. Others, like Bonhoeffer, resisted. When the state church arrangement collapsed in 1918, some theologians faced the prospect that the church would disintegrate into sects equanimously (e.g., Harnack), others turned Romeward (Erik Peterson). Gradually the churches learned to govern themselves and developed a social conscience. Luther's legacy remains a mixed blessing.[10]

Another strain of the Reformation, the Anabaptists, part of the radical wing of the movement, has a closer relation to our theme, the apocalyptic kingdom of God. Baptist history is multinational and ranges from violent insurrection to pacifist nonresistance. We only wish to notice two colorful examples, Thomas Münzer (1490-1525) at Zwickau in Saxony, and John Beukels of Leiden (d. 1536) at Münster in Westphalia. Münzer was a studious priest with a varied pastoral experience when he became pastor in Zwickau. Here he met three men who held a radical Biblicism, yet laid claim to direct revelation due to their possession of the Spirit, and denied infant baptism. They also believed in the millennium. Münzer shared their views, prepared as he was by Joachite

---

[10]Troeltsch's treatment is in his *The Social Teaching of the Christian Churches*, vol. 2 (Chicago: University of Chicago, 1981; orig. ed. 1911), pp. 461-575; Karl Holl, *The Reconstruction of Morality* (Minneapolis: Augsburg, 1979; orig. ed. 1919); idem, *What did Luther Understand by Religion?* (Philadelphia: Fortress, 1977; orig. ed. 1917); the Harnack-Peterson correspondence has been translated from Peterson's *Theologische Traktate* in the *Dublin Review* 226 (1952) 41-57.

influence which he frankly acknowledged. Driven from Zwickau he became pastor in Alstedt. Here he began to denounce Luther as a "scribe" and worse. He rejected even the authority of Scripture, as well as infant baptism, and preached revolt. Violence he justified on account of the nearness of the endtime. The royal priesthood of the common man was now in a position to break the last of the kingdoms of this world, the papal-imperial monarchy. Sovereignty rested in the godly people. He tried to convince miners and magistrates to share their goods equally.

The peasants published their moderate, modernizing demands in Twelve Articles (1525): abolition of serfdom, right to elect pastors, moderate tithes, restoration of fishing, hunting, woodcutting and pasture rights, just work and rent, no extortionist death tax.[11] Revolt spread, with some violence. It will be obvious at once that from a Catholic ecclesial point of view the only objectionable clause in these Articles was the demand to elect pastors, and even that one could have been negotiated, e.g., the bishops could have conceded the peasants' right of refusal or non-reception of a pastor who had been nominated. Indeed, at that time, it was sometimes the case that the lords or the town council had the right to present candidates to the bishop for a pastoral office in their domain. The peasants were only asking to have a voice alongside the nobles and the urban patricians. For the rest, the demands were of a social or economic nature. Münzer now published a pamphlet dedicated to Christ as Duke and King of Kings and to the Church of the poor, his Bride. He preached the imminence of the kingdom of God; the peasants' struggle was a sign of the end. He designed a banner with a rainbow symbolic of the new covenant, since he had come to see in the peasant revolt the end of the fifth monarchy prophesied in Daniel. He placed himself at the head of the rebels.

Philip of Hesse met and defeated the peasants at Frankenhausen. Münzer fled but was captured while hiding. He

[11]Text in *Luther's Works*, vol. 46 (Philadelphia: Fortress, 1967), pp. 8-16.

recanted, took communion, and was beheaded (1525).[12]

In the years 1533-1535 another outbreak occurred in the prosperous prince-bishopric of Münster. Under the leadership of a pastor turned Lutheran, Bernard Rothmann, and a sympathetic mayor, Bernard Knipperdolling, the city was moved toward the Reformation. Rothmann gradually turned from Lutheran to Zwinglian to Anabaptist positions on the sacraments. By January of 1534 his faction was in control. Lutherans and Catholics withdrew and the prince-bishop's hand was momentarily stayed by Philip of Hesse. Sympathizers flocked to the town from the surrounding territory. News of the Anabaptist triumph in Münster reached persecuted Anabaptists in the Netherlands. Two of their apostles took the news as a sign of the start of the millennium. They traveled to Münster posthaste. These Dutch emissaries, John Mathijs of Haarlem and John Beukels, a tailor from Leiden, quickly assumed the leadership of the town council. Mathijs slew a blacksmith who had criticized him on the spot. During his six weeks of rule Mathijs was able to introduce communism of goods and property, both an effort to reproduce the life of the apostolic community and a military necessity. He was killed in a sortie on Easter Sunday.

His place was quickly taken by Beukels. He united church and state in his person and after a victory over the bishop's soldiers had himself crowned king of righteousness, king of the people of God, ruler of the new Zion. He held a messianic banquet in the town square. The kingdom of God on earth had begun in Münster!

One of his oddest decrees was the rivival of Old Testament polygamy. Forty-nine men who opposed this rule were put to death. Women did succeed in getting him to rescind the measure that they had to accept as husband the first man to ask them. Beukel's rule became ever more cruel and oppressive. He beheaded one of his wives when she criticized him and trampled on her body while the rest looked on.

[12]G.H. Williams, *The Radical Reformation* (Philadelphia: Westminster, 1962), pp. 44-84. For Münzer's sermon before the princes, see *Spiritual and Anabaptist Writers*, ed. G.H. Williams (LCC 25; Philadelphia: Westminster, 1957), pp. 47-70.

Two townsmen could stand this no longer. They betrayed a gate to the bishop's men. After a fierce battle the city was taken on 25 June 1535 and almost all the inhabitants slaughtered. Rothmann was probably killed in the battle. Knipperdolling and Beukels were tried and tortured with red-hot tongs. Their bodies were placed in iron cages and suspended from the tower of the Lambertikirche. The cages are still there.[13]

The Anabaptists' stories are most important for our purpose because of all the Reformation groups they alone linked the gospel message of the kingdom of God with socio-political concerns. They were the principal rediscoverers of this theme in this period. Of course the stories we have just told make them appear crazy. But it would be a mistake to dismiss them as unimportant or valueless. This was the easy path taken by the mainstream churches at the time. But the Anabaptists did not die out with these military disasters. They learned from them. They turned from violent revolution to strict pacifism, familiar to Americans from their heirs, the Mennonite, Amish and Brethren peace churches. From ecclesial, liturgical and even biblical points of view they are hardly above criticism. But in their religious positions on social and political structures they have been harbingers of the future, pioneers of a more just social order. This is especially so in their tendencies toward egalitarian democracy, social welfare, and religious liberty and toleration. Even their pacificism may some day soon win a similar universal consensus. The Anabaptists, once so despised and persecuted (they were troublemakers, as we have seen), deserve an honored place in the kingdom story. Nowhere has their influence been greater than in the United States, from Rhode Island on. Contemporary theologians like Jürgen Moltmann hold that the mainstream churches must become more like them.[14]

---

[13] Williams, *Radical Reformation*, pp. 362-386.

[14] See H.S. Bender, *The Anabaptists and Religious Liberty* (Philadelphia: Fortress, 1970) and the interview with Moltmann in *Christian Century* 100.8 (16 March 1983) 248: "The future of the Reformation lies in its left wing."

We now rejoin the line of the classical Reformation with a brief consideration of Bucer and Calvin. Martin Bucer (1491-1551), professional theologian even before his adherence to Luther, was the reformer of Strasbourg and adviser to many reforming states. Driven from the Continent during the Augsburg Interim, Bucer came to England in 1549, where he was received with much honor by the boy king Edward VI and the archbishop of Canterbury Thomas Cranmer. He was made royal professor of theology at Cambridge. Once settled he wrote his most characteristic and last book, *De Regno Christi, On the Kingdom of Christ*. It was written in 1550 for the king in the hope that during his reign the Reformation would be established in England in such a way that it would shape and penetrate the entire life of the nation. The work was published on the Continent in 1557, four years after the king's death, but its ideas may have influenced his policies. Bucer went beyond Luther in that he taught that the whole of human life must be ordered according to the will of God as revealed in the Bible. That was the meaning of the Reformation for him. He also differed from Luther in commenting on the synoptic gospels.

Bucer's *Kingdom of Christ* is a remarkable, detailed blueprint for a Christian society, church and state together, based on a biblical theology. Its two books contain first a theological statement based on Bible, church and sacraments, and then a series of practical proposals formulated as fourteen laws concerning: (1) religious education; (2) Sundays and holidays; (3) church buildings; (4) the ministry; (5) church property; (6) poor relief; (7) marriage and divorce; (8) job training, trade schools; (9) food; (10) civil legislation; (11) civil service; (12) the courts; (13) the penal system; (14) penal law and capital punishment. He tried but failed to keep church property as an endowment for church service. The treatment of marriage is very long because he tried to prove the biblical legitimacy of divorce. His emphasis on schools and education for ministry suggests his Dominican and humanist background. His plan of a Christocracy influenced the Puritans on Sunday laws and Milton on divorce but also the anti-Puritan archbishop of Canterbury John Whitgift.

Bucer's work was dedicated to the king. Thus it comes as no surprise that he understood the kingdom of God according to our third type, the political or Eusebian model. In some ways he was a semiutopian, naively biblical social ethicist, but his policies and proposals did not all fall on deaf ears in the Anglican church and he was not devoid of practical administrative experience. To this extent his achievement is an impressive one.[15]

After Luther, John Calvin of Geneva (1509-1564) was the most directly influential of the Reformers. The kingdom of God is not fully thematized in his great *Institutes of the Christian Religion*, but we give two representative samples: "By proclaiming the kingdom of God, [the Baptist] was calling them to faith, for by the Kingdom of God . . . he meant the forgiveness of sins, salvation, life, and utterly everything that we obtain in Christ." "God reigns where men, both by denial of themselves and by contempt of the world and of earthly life, pledge themselves to his righteousness in order to aspire to a heavenly life. Thus there are two parts to this kingdom: first, that God by the power of his Spirit correct all the desires of the flesh which by squadrons war against him; second, that he shape all our thoughts in obedience to his rule."[16] We can generalize that for Calvin the kingdom can be spiritual blessings, heaven, sometimes the church, but never the papal church, or the state as such or a future divine intervention on earth. Calvin was too preoccupied with constructing a reformed church and a Christian commonwealth and with opposing the Roman church and the Anabaptists to worry much about apocalyptic eschatology.

Nevertheless Calvin's teaching had some significant practical, social effects. He was the first major Christian teacher

[15]Bucer's work is available in English in Wilhelm Pauck, *Melanchthon and Bucer* (LCC 19: Philadelphia: Westminster, 1969), pp. 155-394.

[16]Calvin, *Institutes of the Christian Religion*, ed. J.T. McNeill (LCC 20, 21; Philadelphia: Westminster, 1960), 1.613 (3.3.19) and 2.905 (3.20.42).

to permit usury. This had led some to dub him the founder of capitalism. This is no doubt exaggerated, since this was not his direct intent, but he did shape a religious ethos fitted to an industrious, literate, urban middle class. His church polity was rather aristocratic, limiting the franchise to the board of elders (like a Swiss urban patriciate), but helped to prepare for a conservative type of democratic government characteristic of Swiss and Anglo-Saxon countries. The process was accelerated after Calvin's death when a dispute arose between Pierre Ramus and Theodore Beza on whether the entire congregation had the right to vote. Ramus defended the congregation's right against the elders. Ramus lost in Geneva but his view influenced the English Congregationalists who as pilgrims brought their polity to New England, thus helping to shape the American future.[17]

Calvin's stress on a disciplined Christian life and the synoptic gospels had an effect not only on his own direct heirs, but also, after the carnage of the Thirty Years War, on Lutheran spiritual practice. This movement, called Pietism, had an initial impact on Frankfurt and Saxony, before spreading to Württemberg and Moravia. Our concern is with the Württemberg form of Pietism, because its leaders, Johann Albrecht Bengel (1687-1752) and Friedrich Christoph Oetinger (1702-1782), developed it in the direction of eschatological speculation and an interest in biblical prophecy. Bengel, besides a pithy commentary on the whole New Testament, wrote a commentary on the Apocalypse entitled *The Revelation of John or Rather of Jesus Christ Declared* (1740). This contained an apocalyptic chronology coordinating events of world history with the biblical text.[18]

---

[17]J. Moltmann. "Zur Bedeutung des P. Ramus für Philosophie und Theologie im Calvinismus," *ZKG* 68 (1957) 295-310; Troeltsch, *Social Teachings,* 2.576-691, has a very positive evaluation of the social effects of Calvinism. It occurs to the present writer that, in political practice, American Roman Catholics, influenced by Thomistic social thought and Irish clan traditions, as well as by their Protestant environment, have adopted a similar philosophy of government since about 1880. Democratizing church structures remains a matter of current discussion.

[18]See the translation in P.C. Erb, *Pietists: Selected Writings* (New York: Paulist, 1983), pp. 272-4.

Oetinger combined this sort of apocalyptic interest with a mystical-theosophical view of nature derived from Jacob Boehme and influenced by Emanuel Swedenborg. Direct influences of these thinkers on Immanuel Kant are difficult to establish. What we know for certain is that Kant's parents were simple, hard-working people and devout Pietists. Kant grew up in a Pietist home. From this it is safe to conclude that the Kants read the Bible regularly and were interested in a holy life according to a pattern provided in the synoptic gospels. Beyond this they *may* have been interested in biblical prophecy in the Pietist style but this must remain only a possibility.

II. Enlightenment, Counter-Enlightenment, Romanticism, Positivism

The philosophy typical of the late seventeenth and of the eighteenth centuries is rationalistic, based on mathematical models. This is true for Descartes, Spinoza, Leibniz, Wolff. English philosophy at the same time moved from sensism (Locke) through empiricism (Hobbes, Berkeley) to skepticism (Hume). That is the main road of the Enlightenment, hostile to myth and loose speculation, weak, so it is said, on a historical sense. But soon there was a counter-movement, represented by Voltaire and Rousseau, Hamann and Jacobi, Vico and Herder. These last two were most important in re-evaluating the human truth contained in the early myths, sagas and early poetry of the peoples of the world. They are pioneers in the modern philosophy of history. Tempting though it be, we will not treat them in detail because they do not address the kingdom of God theme directly. But we note that, together with the rationalists, they make up the immediate thought-world in which Kant operated.[19]

[19]See Karl Löwith, *Meaning in History* (Chicago: University of Chicago, 1949), for Vico and Voltaire, pp. 104-136; and, especially, Isaiah Berlin, *Vico and Herder* (New York: Viking, 1976), and his *Against the Current* (New York: Viking, 1980), esp. pp. 1-80, 111-130, 162-188.

Immanuel Kant (1724-1804), born in Königsberg, East Prussia, today Kaliningrad in the Soviet Union, is better known as a philosopher than as a theologian, and with good reason. In the academic procession which opened the school year he kept his place till it reached the church door. Then he dropped out and walked home. There was no place for prayer in his philosophy. He undermined the rationalists' proofs for the existence of God. Nevertheless, in his old age he turned to religious philosophy in a short work provocatively entitled *Religion Within the Limits of Reason Alone* (1793). Religious issues continued to interest him till his death eleven years later, but this is his principal work in the area. The book has four chapters. The first deals with original sin as radical evil. Original sin was a church doctrine which the Enlightenment thought it had laughed out of court. It is characteristic of Kant's courageous independence of mind that he could find purely rational meaning in it. The second chapter deals with Christology, but never mentions Jesus Christ! It refers to him as "the personified idea of the good principle." The third chapter ("book three") is entitled "The victory of the Good over the Evil Principle, and the Founding of a Kingdom of God on Earth." This is the crucial chapter for our theme. The fourth chapter is a kind of anti-clerical ecclesiology.

Kant begins his book three with a recognition that evil is caused not only by our individual uncontrolled passions but also by society. This social evil can be overcome, he says, by a social alliance called an *ethical commonwealth* or a *kingdom of virtue*, analogous to a political state or commonwealth. The kingdom is an "ethical commonwealth under divine moral legislation" and Kant calls this commonwealth a church. Kant's presentation is in fact somewhat confused, having affinities with both the spiritual-mystical and ecclesial models. Yet, at least in words, he keeps open the hope of an eschatological divine completion of our human efforts.

For Kant there are four signs or notes of this church: 1. universality and oneness; 2. purity or holiness; 3. the freedom proper to a republic; 4. an unchangeable constitution, which he compares to that of a family or household, thereby denying its political character. (Living in the Prussian state church world, he seems to have wanted to keep the two separate.) Though he says that its constitution must not change, he does allow of alteration in details.

Kant is at his best in the following passage:

> To found a moral people of God is ... a task whose consummation can be looked for not from men but only from God Himself. Yet man is not entitled on this account to be idle in this business and to let Providence rule, as though each could apply himself exclusively to his own private moral affairs and relinquish to a higher wisdom all the affairs of the human race (as regards its moral destiny). Rather must man proceed as though everything depended upon him; only on this condition dare he hope that higher wisdom will grant the completion of his well-intentioned endeavors. The wish of all well-disposed people is, therefore, "the kingdom of God come, that His will be done on earth." But what preparations must they now make that it shall come to pass?"[20]

We may quarrel with Kant's theology of grace in this passage, especially his idea that we must act "as if" all depended on us. For faith, all really does depend upon God, both now and in the future, and yet he calls us to obedience. There is no "as if." But Kant's general drift is in the right direction.

Though his conception of the kingdom lacks the benefits of historical exegesis and the details are muddy, there can be no doubt that Kant thought that the kingdom theme was important. He made it the center of his religious thought, and, because his own thinking was so influential, it has occupied the center of theological reflection ever since, apart from a few short periods. In this sense, as we said at the beginning of this chapter, he is the hero of the story, along with Johannes Weiss and a few present day theologians.

[20]Kant, *Religion* (New York: Harper, 1960).

By way of negative criticism, we need to recognize that Kant reduces the kingdom of God and Christianity itself, for all practical purposes, to morality and conscience, because he was so hostile to actual church institutions and because he was so deistical. His Pelagian, de-eschatologized concept of the kingdom (i.e., we build the kingdom ourselves and thus save ourselves) dominated the nineteenth century, only to have its Social Gospel illusions shattered in the first World War. We do not pretend to have done justice to the many fine nuances in Kant's thought, but only to have pointed out his overall effect.

Before rushing on to other philosophical figures, let us pause briefly to glance at two early theological responses to Kant, one Protestant, one Catholic. The first is Friedrich Schleiermacher (1768-1834). In 1799, that is, within six years of the publication of Kant's work, the Christian church had a doughty young David in the person of this thirty-one year old theologian, ready with a deft response. Schleiermacher's *On Religion: Speeches to its Cultured Despisers* attempted a Sturm und Drang correction to Kant's ice-cold moralism by defining religion as a feeling of absolute dependence. He rightly fought for a place for feeling, emotion, beauty, ecstasy in religion. To his critics he, as well as Kant, gave too little place to intellect, truth, doctrine. But that is not our concern here. Schleiermacher mentions the kingdom of God six times in his first work, the only one we will consider, but it is nearly impossible to pin him down as to its meaning, since he writes in a rather opaque style. Thus, "[Jesus] who first conceived the idea of the kingdom of God, from which, if from anything in the sphere of religion, a system might have been produced to the new mystics or enthusiasts ... in whom, perhaps, an original beam of the inner light still shines."[21]

Our first Catholic respondent to Kant is Bernard Galura (1764-1856), less well known than Schleirmacher but more lucid. He died as prince-bishop of Brixen, at 92, after a long

[21]Scheleiermacher, *On Religion* (New York: Harper, 1958), p. 17. Other references: pp. 7, 143, 145, 152, 264.

life of pastoral service. His greatest challenge came to him from 1791 to 1805, when, having just finished his doctorate, he was made city pastor of Freiburg im Breisgau, just in time to face the French Revolution and the war with Napoleon. He was never happier or more productive. For, in the midst of this turmoil, he produced a catechetical theology in six volumes![22] Its key theme was the kingdom of God which he used as an organizing principle which would be biblically based and easy to use in preaching. This is how Galura thinks:

> The system of religion is the glorious edifice of the faith of Christians ... This system must necessarily be found in the Bible; it must be a thought therein around which Jesus' whole plan revolves; ... this thought is the kingdom of God; this teaching around which the whole of religion turns as verily around its center is the teaching of the Bible on the kingdom of God. If I gather together all the statements of the Lord and the Apostle, they all have one and indeed the following thought: Christians! There is a kingdom of God, a kingdom of imperishable beatitude; should all the kingdoms of the world perish, one does not, God's kingdom. The Father in heaven offers you his kingdom and the happiness of his kingdom. (NTC 1, p. 9, 11)

The idea of the kingdom of God became Galura's life-principle, the principle of his kerygmatic theology and the center of his preaching. To be sure, this idea in his writings is not only many-layered but also has many meanings. On the one hand this kingdom is understood as people, as Christians, the saints and even the angels; on the other hand this kingdom appears to be divided up into social regions: "the kingdom of God over the Son" and "the kingdom of God

---

[22]*Neueste Theologie des Christentums* (Augsburg, 1800-1804). My knowledge of and citations from Galura come from Günter Biemer, in H. Fries and G. Schwaiger, *Katholische Theologen Deutschlands im 19. Jahrhundert*, 3 vols (Munich: Kösel, 1975), 1.227-252.

under the Son" (NTC II, p. 141; VI, pp. 382). It is the kingdom of the virtuous, it is "itself virtue and man's salvation"(II, p. 173). It has finally an eschatological dimension, when at the end "heaven and earth make up a single kingdom of God" (IV, pp. 231). The purpose and goal of this kingdom is the beatitude of human beings. Though an Enlightenment man, "he knew the positive side of the ambivalent concept and motivation of the Enlightenment and admitted: "True enlightenment consists in this, that we view everything in its true light; we do this when we consider everything in the light of the kingdom of God" (NTC V, pp. xxxix). Galura was a man of one idea.

It is commonly said that nineteenth century thought falls into a tidy division: 1800-1850 romantic idealism; 1851-1900 positivism.[23] Although this is a little too simple, there is a change noticeable after the failed revolution of 1848. The dominant thinkers after the sober Kant are the romantic philosopher F.W.J. Schelling (1775-1854) and his seminary classmate G.W.F. Hegel (1770-1831) who attempted a synthesis of romantic enlightenment viewpoints. Although both these thinkers were interested in religious problems, the religious thinking of this period tended to center on the category of the Spirit, to speculate on the meaning of the Trinity, and, for these two reasons, to remain closest to the Fourth Gospel.[24] But, after Kant, the kingdom could not be entirely ignored. In fact it emerges at the culmination of the religious systems of both thinkers. We will look first at some of their scattered remarks and then notice their final treatments of the theme. A nice way to begin is with a closing exclamation to a new year's letter Hegel sent to Schelling in 1795. "May the kingdom of God come, and our hands not be idle in the

---

[23]Bernhard Welte, "Zum Strukturwandel der katholischen Theologie im 19. Jahrhundert," in his collected essays *Auf der Spur des Ewigen* (Freiburg im Breisgau: Herder, 1965), pp. 380-409; Maurice Mandelbaum, *History, Man, and Reason: A Study in 19th Century Thought* (Baltimore: Johns Hopkins, 1971), pp. 3-37, tries to correct this division a little. Welte's article remains a classic.

[24]W.A. Schulze, "Das Johannesevangelium im deutschen Idealismus," *Zeitschrift für philosophische Forschung* 18 (1964) 85-118.

lap!"[25] Full of the Promethean-Faustian spirit of the times, when the philosophical wits thought they were the mind of God, Hegel here imagines his friend and himself as agents at the birth of the kingdom of God. Not bad for a twenty-four year old who has just described Fichte as a titan, and whose world was being transformed by the French Revolution. Their slogan was "We don't want to remain behind!" In a similar vein, his friend Friedrich Schlegel wrote, "The revolutionary desire to realize the kingdom of God is the flexible starting point of progressive education and the principle of modern history."[26] Schelling joins the chorus: "It is customary to say, man's will is his kingdom of heaven, and it is true, if the pure naked will alone is understood by this. For only the man who would be transported into pure willing would be free of all nature."[27] These brief remarks all reflect a certain intoxication with the power of speculative thought. In another early work, *On University Studies* (1802), Schelling is contrasting Christianity with classical paganism. His main point is that pagan polytheism sees God in nature and space, whereas Christianity finds God disclosed primarily in time, in history, as a moral kingdom. "That which the Greek religion had as simultaneity Christianity has as succession in time, although it has not yet achieved its definitive form ... the divine unveils itself in the ideal world - above all, in history; here the mystery of the divine kingdom is disclosed."[28]

By taking seriously biblical revelation in historical event

[25] *Briefe von und an Hegel*, ed. J. Hoffmeister, vol. I: 1785-1812 (Hamburg: Meiner, 1961), p. 18: "Das Reich Gottes komme, und unsre Hände seien nicht müssig im Schosse!" It has been observed that Hegel was the first major metaphysician since Aristotle to have married. This could help to understand the metaphor. Shortly after this in the same letter Hegel adds: "Reason and freedom remain our solution, and our gathering point the invisible church."

[26] *Athenäumsfragmente*, No. 222.

[27] *The Ages of the World* (New York: Columbia Univ. Press, 1942), p. 123. This work was written 1811-12, but not published till 1861.

[28] Schelling, *On University Studies* (Athens, Ohio: Ohio University Press, 1966), pp. 82-85 and 158.

and word, understood as God's reign gradually establishing itself and transfiguring the world, Schelling and Hegel did achieve something important. They attempted to introduce time and history into the static, eternal structures of Greek metaphysics. This was a philosophical démarche of the highest order as well as a preparation for Darwin's and Newman's perception of evolution in nature and church doctrine. From our point of view, it broke the static conviction that society was irreformable, that things must continue sunk in original sin and total depravity until we reach heaven itself. By taking the Bible as seriously as metaphysics they could see the hand of God active in history on the move.

After Hegel succeeded Fichte as professor of philosophy at the university of Berlin (he would have preferred to stay in southern Germany but the authorities there would not trust him), he gave a lecture series four times on the philosophy of religion before his sudden death in the cholera epidemic of 1831. Working from student transcripts, one of Hegel's Berlin colleagues, the theologian Philipp Marheineke, got out an edition of these lectures the year after Hegel's death. The third part of this large work is about revelatory, consummate, absolute religion and turns out to be a philosophical interpretation of Christianity organized into three parts. The first is entitled The Kingdom of the Father and treats mainly the doctrine of the Triune God. The second, The Kingdom of the Son, treats the fall, the incarnation, the teaching, death and resurrection of Christ. The third part, The Kingdom of the Spirit, treats the doctrine of the church, the sacraments and Christian life. Thus we see that the very arrangement of the work focuses on the kingdom of the Triune God.[29]

In this work Hegel's teaching on the kingdom itself is

---

[29]We use the outstandingly readable and practical interim study edition of this work in translation by P.C. Hodgson: Hegel, *The Christian Religion* (Chico, CA: Scholars Press, 1979), as a guide to the Lasson edition of the German. A final form should appear soon from the University of California Press, Berkeley. Hegel explains his structure on pp. 38f., and cf. the note on p. 44.

somewhat bewildering, in part because it is so central that it must be everything. Most of the detailed explanations come in the subsection on the teaching of Christ. Here is a sample of his remarks:

> This universal ground [in the teaching of Christ] is the *heavenly kingdom*, the kingdom of God—a substantial, intelligible world in which all values are cast away that are sought in earthly, mundane things. This is not God alone, the One, but rather a *kingdom* of God, the eternal as a home for Spirit, the eternal as the dwelling place of subjectivity. This elevation is brought before the imagination with infinite energy, summoning and inciting the interiority of disposition (p. 185).
> Jesus' proclamation of the kingdom is, so to speak, sansculottism, or in oriental terms, revolutionary (p. 188).
> This is the kingdom of God, which has been taught by Christ: it is the real divinity, God in his existence, spiritual actuality, the kingdom of heaven. This divine reality already contains within itself God and his kingdom the community; this is a concrete content, and it is the major content (p. 192f).
> The new religion expresses itself as a new consciousness, the consciousness of a reconciliation of humanity with God. This reconciliation, expressed as a state of affairs, is the kingdom of God, an actuality (p. 194).

For Hegel this new religion is the kingdom of God (p. 195). When he begins to speak of the Kingdom of the Spirit he describes it as a "living, spiritual life, a divine community," as "the first, eternal Idea," as "Spirit determining itself in terms of the universal and passing over into actuality," in the life of Jesus (p. 199). It is the presence of God in us, our relationship to God himself (p. 216f). Later he says, "The church is the kingdom of God, the achieved presence, life, preservation, and enjoyment of Spirit" (p. 260). Finally, it is a "mystical union, the implicit unity of divine and human nature" (p. 270).

To put it simply, for Hegel the kingdom is everywhere. It

is the center of Christ's preaching and offers the vision of a community of God and humanity. It is a cipher for the Christian religion. Hegel recognizes its revolutionary potential. Since, in his ethical work *Philosophy of Right*, he comes close to identifying the Absolute in history with the state, by calling the church the kingdom of God he is in fact making the state the kingdom, because for him the church is only a subordinate department of the state.[30] Thus we see that Hegel interprets the kingdom in three of our patristic ways: spiritual-mystical, political and ecclesial. What is missing is the apocalyptic.

After Hegel's sudden death Schelling was called to Berlin from Munich. There he was having a great influence on the circle of Catholic intellectuals connected with the recently founded University of Munich.[31] Schelling came to Berlin full of foreboding. He knew he would have a hard time filling Hegel's shoes and meeting the diverse expectations of his illustrious auditors. He tried hard in his last major lecture series, *The Philosophy of Revelation* (1841). At the time the lectures did not please his most critical listeners but have long been recognized as a major contribution to the philosophy of religion in Germany and elsewhere. Their neglect and lack of translation in the English world has prevented them from having much influence in that world except very indirectly through Tillich. They are structured into two main parts: the philosophy of myths, an effort to interpret myths and world religions sympathetically. The second part is a philosophical interpretation of Christianity. In the famous and final thirty-sixth lecture he summarizes his whole approach, which is philosophically to find the truth in Christianity and to reconcile it with thought. Then his thoughts turn to the future form of Christianity and to eschatology. If Christianity is to be adequate to the task of being *the* world religion of modern times it must develop

---

[30] Hegel, *Philosophy of Right* (New York: Oxford University Press, 1952), p. 156 the state as the absolute; pp. 165-174 church and state.

[31] T.F. O'Meara, *Romantic Idealism and Roman Catholicism: Schelling and the Theologians* (Notre Dame: University of Notre Dame, 1982).

into a completely self-conscious human knowledge, to include universal scientific knowledge. Does the New Testament provide for such future stages of development?

Schelling finds his positive answer in the characters of three apostles: Peter, Paul, and John. Peter is the apostle of the Father and represents the Roman Catholic church or the first millennium and a half of christendom; Paul is the apostle of the Son and represents Protestantism; John is the apostle of the Spirit and represents the church of the future, the perfect religion of mankind. Little wonder that some of Schelling's hearers thought they were witnessing the birth of a new religion in the lecture hall, since Schelling's description of the church of the Spirit sounds much like his own brand of romantic idealism.

Let us add a word on Schelling's sources and influence. Schelling was delighted when he later found out from Neander's church history that his scheme had been anticipated by Joachim of Fiore, although for Joachim the first *status* refers to the Old Testament era. Schleiermacher, in his *The Christian Faith* (1822), had already linked the Roman Catholic Church with Peter and Protestantism with Paul. Once Schelling has singled out John as the gospel of the spiritual future, this was taken up in various ways. The Broad Church movement in England made John the gospel of English modernism and even drew up a creed in Johannine phraseology. Vladimir Solovyev, a Russian lay theologian present at the original Berlin lectures, thought he saw in his own Eastern Orthodoxy a concrete realization of the Johannine church of the Spirit, at least in germ or ideally. He went on to work for the renewal of his church in this sense. There were also German listeners whose dreams found an expression in the term, the Third Reich, although they never intended what came.[32]

Now that we have completed our report on Hegel and Schelling and their use of the kingdom motif, we return

---

[32]*Schellings Werke*, ed. M. Schröter (Munich: Beck, 1965), 6.686-704; this is summarized in English in Karl Löwith, *Meaning in History* (Chicago: University, 1949), pp. 208-212.

briefly to southern Germany to pick up the impact of their ideas on some Catholic theological thinkers. The dark genius of German Catholic idealism was the lay theologian Franz von Baader (1765-1841). Between 1828 and 1838 he gave his own *Lectures on Speculative Dogmatics*. In this strange long work of chiliastic mysticism, "Baader chose as his leitmotif the kingdom of God. The system will have four parts: the ground of the kingdom, its destruction and return, its continuation in history, its fulfillment in eternal life."[33]

The founder of the Catholic Tübingen school of theology was Johann Sebastian von Drey (1777-1853). From the very beginning of his activity as a teacher of systematic theology he stressed that the unifying principle of all Christian thought must be the kingdom of God. In his *Brief Introduction to the Study of Theology* (1819) he said:

> Through the absolute necessity and truth which the idea of a kingdom of God has for reason, all manifestations of the kingdom in the history of humanity, all the teachings of Christianity which disclose and declare the mysteries (the plan and the organization of the kingdom) in the history of humanity, attain the same character of necessity and truth. As Christ himself manifestly transformed the entire history of antiquity into ideas, and his apostles did the same, so does scientific theology in its turn transform the story of Christ himself into pure ideas, and thereby joins necessary ideas and the story of Christ into a unified whole.[34]

Drey here wants to employ the idea of the kingdom of God as the conceptual link between the necessary, universal, eternal truths of philosophy and the scandalously contingent,

---

[33]O'Meara, *Romantic Idealism*, p. 136.

[34]Drey, *Kurze Einleitung in das Studium der Theologie* (Tübingen: Laupp, 1819; repr. Darmstadt: Wissenschaftliche Buchgesellschaft, 1971), #65, p. 41. Cf. Josef Rief, *Reich Gottes und Gesellschaft nach J.S. Drey und J.B. Hirscher* (Paderborn: Schoningh, 1965).

particular and time-bound truths of biblical revelation and church doctrine. He presupposes from Kant that the idea of a kingdom of God is a necessity of reason itself (as the ethical commonwealth). But, like Hegel and Schelling, he wants to link being and time, reason and revelation. A theology organized around the concept of the kingdom of God is, for Drey, that link. The kingdom is the bridge. Drey also worked on the concept of a Christian socialism in his *Apologetics*. In this concern for the social implications of the kingdom he was as one with his Tübingen colleague, the moral theologian Johann Baptist Hirscher (1788-1865).

Hirscher's principal work was *Christian Morality as the Doctrine of the Realization of the Divine Kingdom in Humanity* in three volumes (first edition 1835-1836; fifth 1851).

Hirscher's first "book" in this work is entitled: "The idea of the kingdom of heaven in itself and objectively, as well as its opposite, the satanic kingdom." This is an interesting way to begin and allows him to consider evil as part of the picture. But already we detect a mistake. Misled by Matthew's idiom he takes "kingdom of *heaven*" as his starting point. This damages his definition, even though he is trying to build on the synoptic gospels.

> This kingdom is over us (as its name expresses) in heaven; and has drawn near to earth from there. If we then look for information on it, we must turn our gaze upward. Thence shall we be instructed also in the event when he calls the kingdom which he has come to earth to found the kingdom of his Father and the kingdom of heaven (Matt 4:17; 5:3, 10, 19; 6:10; Luke 11:2; 22:29, etc.); when he asseverates that he has come here exclusively to proclaim and to effect what he has heard from the Father, what he has seen there from him, and as he has been commissioned by him (John 1:18; 3:13, 32, 34; 6:46, 8:28, 42; 7:16; 12:49, 50, etc.); and when he finally demands that the will of the Father be done precisely here below, just as it is done in heaven (Matt 6:10). So we gaze above. And upon whom must our eyes fall above all if not upon its

creator and king-God. In him the kingdom has reality now; through him its nature; in him its head.[35]

On this basis, a jumble of biblical concepts, Hirscher constructed a moderately coherent and progressive morality of church, state and family.

These groping efforts were not without their positive results on the wider church. The activist priest Adolph Kolping (1813-1865) began his workingmen's associations in Cologne in the following decades and they soon spread throughout Germany. This success, and the pressure from rising socialism, aroused the courageous archbishop of Mainz, Wilhelm Emmanuel von Ketteler (1811-1877), primate of the German church, to write his *The Worker Question and Christianity* (1864). After the unification of Germany under Bismarck an eight-year period of persecution of the church began, the battle of cultures. This prevented more from being accomplished in the social realm, but Catholics learned to organize politically, forging the Center Party into a significant parliamentary tool. They survived. After the death of the social reactionary Pius IX, Ketteler's pioneer work bore fruit in the first positive papal social encyclical letter, *Rerum Novarum*, on the condition of labor, issued by Leo XIII in 1891. Workers' right to organize for collective bargaining was recognized. Summing up, it is clear that these pioneering modern Catholic theologians saw the fruitfulness of the kingdom idea as an organizing principle but were lacking in their appreciation of its earthly eschatological realization as an act of God.

After the failed revolutions of 1848 there was a certain indigestion with idealistic speculation. People grew hungry once again for plain facts. This is the turn to positivism in nineteenth century thought. Technical science embarked on new triumphs. Detailed historical works took the place of sweeping sketches. It was the heyday of textual criticism in biblical studies. Politically conservative leaders tried to

---

[35] Hirscher, *Die Christliche Moral als Lehre von der Verwirklichung des göttlichen Reiches in der Menschheit* (Tübingen: Laupp, 1835), #23, p. 80f.

distract their people from the temptation to socialism by nationalist unifications (Italy and Germany) and the establishment of colonial empires. Intellectually it was the era of the triumph of neo-Kantian moralism. Trinitarian speculation fell out of favor, and so did Christology. Religion was once again turned into "work for the kingdom of God." Indeed, it was thought that with a little effort the whole world could be won for Christ in a single generation. Such a mass conversion would be accompanied by a regeneration which would realize the kingdom of God on earth. Foreign and "inner" or home missions were the order of the day. It was the time of the Social Gospel, the Christian side of the progressivist era, muscular Christianity and bearing the white man's burden to the "lesser breeds without the law." This Culture-Protestantism is still visible in churches built in that period which resemble lecture halls - not without reason since that is what they were often used for, because Christianity was understood as the spiritual aspect of civil society. The whole enterprise, which was not without its noble achievements, came crashing down in the first World War and its aftermath. This crash was the bitter aftertaste of the Pelagian understanding of the kingdom which is the Kantian inheritance.

We want to look now at a few significant representatives of this period. In Germany the main figures are Albrecht Ritschl (1822-1889) and his better known disciple Adolf von Harnack (1851-1930). Although Ritschl's main theological decisions have been enormously influential in Protestantsm, viz., no metaphysics, no mysticism, no Pietism, his name and works are less well known than his ideas. These live on not only through theological followers but also through millions of people who were shaped by the religion textbook he was asked to write for German high schools (1875). A densely concentrated little work, *Instruction in the Christian Religion* is organized around four points: 1. Concerning the kingdom of God (the Father); 2. Concerning reconciliation through Christ; 3. Concerning the Christian life; 4. Concerning public worship. (The last two are related to the Spirit and treat of virtues, church and sacraments.) The kingdom is defined at the outset as follows:

> The kingdom of God is the divinely ordained highest good of the community founded through God's revelation in Christ; but it is the highest good only in the sense that it forms at the same time the ethical ideal for whose attainment the members of the community bind themselves to each other through a definite type of reciprocal action. This meaning of the concept "kingdom of God" becomes clear through the imperative which is simultaneously expressed in it.[36]

In this we have not gotten very far from Kant's ethical commonwealth and categorical imperative. The ethical seriousness and social bonding and activism inherent in this ideal are praiseworthy. But there is little hint of divine grace now and none of divine activity in the future. Ritschl at least kept the kingdom close to Christ and the church. His contemporary, Richard Rothe (1799-1867) made it directly a state organism.[37]

The pebble which would topple the Ritschlian giant had already been hurled, by Johannes Weiss in 1892 (see the next chapter), when the great scholar and historian of dogma Adolf Harnack ushered in the new century by summing up the old in his classic *What is Christianity? (Das Wesen des Christentums,* 1900).[38] This work became an international bestseller and spread the Ritschlian gospel throughout the world without ever mentioning Ritschl's name.

Because of the challenges of the time (socialism and Nietzschean right-wing radical rejection of Christianity) and

---

[36]A. Ritschl, *Three Essays*, trans. Philip Hefner (Philadelphia: Fortress, 1972), p. 222.

[37]Christian Walther, "Der Reich-Gottes-Begriff in der Theologie Richard Rothes und Albrecht Ritschls," *Kerygma und Dogma* 2 (1956) 115-138.

[38](New York: Harper, 1957). References will be to this edition. Cf. K.H. Neufeld, *A. Harnacks Konflikt mit der Kirche* (Innsbruck: Tyrolia, 1979).

the loftiness of his ambition (to save the educated modern world for Christ), Harnack decides from the outset to take the high ground, which some would call a retreat into vague spirituality. Thus he defines the Christian religion as "something simple and sublime; it means one thing and one thing only: Eternal life in the midst of time, by the strength and under the eyes of God" (p. 8). It must not be judged by its ethical or social usefulness. So when he comes to define the kingdom of God (on p. 62) we are not surprised to find him building on the psychological-mystical verse (Luke 17:21).

> The kingdom has a triple meaning. Firstly, it is something supernatural, a gift from above, not a product of ordinary life. Secondly, it is a purely religious blessing, the inner link with the living God. Thirdly, it is the most important experience that a man can have, that on which everything else depends; it permeates and dominates his whole existence, because sin is forgiven and misery banished.

Harnack then goes on to reduce Jesus' message to two doctrines: "God as the Father, and the human soul so ennobled that it can and does unite with him" (p. 63). This message contains no legal or particular elements. It has come into popular American piety as the anagram BOMFOG: the brotherhood of man under the fatherhood of God, familiar to us from the speeches of Governor Nelson Rockefeller of New York. Fed on such an ethereal diet, Harnack found himself unable to resist the importunities of the Kaiser when the time of testing came. In late 1914, when the German government feared it was losing the propaganda war after the destruction of the Louvain library, it asked Harnack, who was head of the Prussian Academy of Sciences, to head a list of signatories to a statement asserting that Germany's war was a cultural war. Harnack complied. In the eyes of his non-German disciples like the Swiss Karl Barth it was the definitive sign that this kind of socially uncritical liberal theology was bankrupt. It was the end of an era.[39]

We have already mentioned the challenges of socialism and Nietzschean aristocratic radicalism. We must now say a word about Marx and Nietzsche. Neither speaks directly about the kingdom, yet their thinking so determines the succeeding eras and is so deeply involved with eschatology that they become an indispensible part of our story.

As a student of the left Hegelian Ludwig Feuerbach, Karl Marx (1818-1883) intended to stand Hegel's emphasis on the spirit on its head, by emphasizing matter. He attempted to overcome utopian socialism (Saint Simon, Fourier, Proudhon) with a "scientific" socialism grounded in economic analysis. By unmasking the economic hypocrisy of bourgeois Christendom (as Freud was later to unmask the sexual hypocrisy), he compelled thoughtful Christians to face the human cost of the industrial revolution with greater urgency. From our point of view his most important contribution was to effect a crucial shift in many people's expectations from a heavenly spiritual salvation to a classless society in this world. Marx expressed himself with harsh animus and anti-religious bias (derived from Feuerbach and made worse by his associate Engels), as well as with a professional arrogance that was not always justified by the correctness of his analysis or his predictions. What is undeniable is that he provided a powerful stimulus for Christians to recover the earthly dimensions of their kingdom hope. To do otherwise would be for them to abandon all hope for this world to atheists.

As Marxian socialism became a major political force in Germany in the 1870's, Bismarck first tried to outlaw it while stealing its practical legislative thunder (royal-imperial military socialism from above). But this did not prevent its growth. The upper classes viewed its rise with mounting

[39]Wilfried Härle, "Der Aufruf der 93 Intellektuellen und Karl Barths Bruch mit der liberalen Theologie," *ZTK* 72 (1975) 207-224, prints the text, lists the theologian signers, e.g., A. Deissmann, W. Hermann, A. Schlatter, R. Seeberg and three Roman Catholics, and provides background and a revisionist critique of Barth's version of the affair's meaning.

horror and dismay. At first they tried to use Christianity as an ideological weapon against it. But this was a broken reed, because the prophets and Jesus were too obviously on the side of the oppressed. The Beatitudes could not be forced into an aristocratic mold. In this dilemma Friedrich Nietzsche (1844-1900) arose as the creator of a new pagan ideology that would hold back the socialists. Nietzsche was a genius, even if an erratic one and eventually a mad one. As a genius he saw deeply into the cause of the problem. He realized that part of the problem was eschatology, a conviction about the future direction and meaning of the historical process. So long as lower class people believed in a better future, whether brought by God, biological evolution, enlightenment progress, or social revolution, they would not stay quietly in their place. Clearheadedly he cut the problem at its root. He got rid of all eschatology. He rejected Christianity as a slave religion, which only expressed the resentment of the under-class. He glorified martial strength, heroic force and amoral willfulness, with the aid of social Darwinism's "survival of the fittest." Hence the superman becomes the goal. Christianity was to be replaced by a return to paganism: classical paganism's myth of the eternal return of all things; Teutonic paganism's pessimistic twilight of the gods (Wagner). Löwith has shrewdly observed that classical paganism was still happy without an eschatology (because it knew no better). But Nietzsche's neopagan myth becomes unhappy, something he describes with horror as "the death of God," or, as we might say, the death of hope for the future.[40]

Nietzsche was a very refined, learned and urbane thinker. It is ironic that the man who would attempt to realize his ideas most energetically and to turn back the tide of Bolshevism should have been such a coarse, petty thinker who probably never read him. (Nietzsche's apologists plead that Hitler grossly misunderstood him. Perhaps so, but to this reader the genetic connection, while certainly not the only necessary one (cf. Thomas Mann's *Reflections of An Unpolitical Man*), is nevertheless patent and undeniable.)

[40]Löwith, *Meaning in History*, pp. 214-222.

It is not our purpose to deny that Nietzsche has many acute and valid insights. We only want to show that he is a consistent, clear-headed example of the rejection of all this-worldly, future-oriented eschatology, and is so precisely because he wants to avoid social justice.

Before we leave the nineteenth century we must still look at developments in Britain and the United States. The Victorian era was a lively one in the Church of England, but the kingdom theme did not especially occupy either the Low Church party which was primarily interested in individual salvation (although evangelicals like William Wilberforce achieved great things socially, like emancipating the slaves throughout the British Empire peacefully) or the High Church movement which was principally concerned with a renewal of the inner life, authority and worship of the church. Our selective approach must fall this time upon a figure often associated with the Broad Church or liberal branch of Anglicanism, Frederick Denison Maurice (1805-1872), although he himself avoided all party labels. Both the title of his principal work, *The Kingdom of Christ* (1838), and his involvement in the Christian Socialist movement (1848-1853) and in a Working Men's College (1854-1872) qualify him for inclusion here.

Maurice's way into the church was an unusual one. He was raised in a devout Unitarian home and converted after his university studies. He received ordination in 1834. Soon thereafter he was encouraged by friends to take a stand on some issues disturbing the church. He realized shrewdly enough that to take on the Tractarians directly and on their own ground would put his position in a bad light. He would appear a weak Christian. So he chose another ground. His *Kingdom of Christ* was subtitled "Hints to a Quaker concerning the Principle, Constitution and Ordinances of the Catholic Church" and originally took the form of a series of letters to a Quaker. In comparison to Quakers, Unitarians and German liberals, Maurice would appear a strong churchman. The plan of the book is to discuss the doctrines in turn of the Quakers, continental Protestants, Unitarians, and Catholics English and Roman, as well as the flaws in each system. He then goes on to sketch his visionof a divine order which finds expression, after the family and the nation, in a universal and spiritual society. This church society or kingdom of Christ has as its signs, baptism, the creeds, forms of worship, the eucharist, the ministry, and scripture. He concludes with a defense of the Church of England as a legitimate national embodiment of this spiritual society.

It will be obvious that this view of the kingdom has affinities with both Eusebius and Augustine. But the use of Scripture (in Part II, Chapter 3) allows us to discern affinities with the spiritual-mystical view (Maurice was especially drawn to the gospel and letters of John and to Plato) and the absence of an apocalyptic dimension. The Old Testament is important to him as grounding the national aspect. Maurice's prose is often opaque and his treatment of the New Testament doctrine of the kingdom tortuous and subtle. But finally he rejects hope of an outward and visible divine kingdom here on earth, on the grounds that what is true in it is already realized or realizable "now as it ever can be in any future period."[41]

Fortunately Maurice did not confine himself to theory but, in the wake of the brutal suppression of the Chartist Movement in 1848, he started a movement for unskilled workers, in collaboration with J.M.F. Ludlow, Charles Kingsley, Jules Lechevalier and Edward Neale. Meetings, publications, classes, unions and campaigns for legislation soon followed, as did extreme hostility. Maurice was deprived of his professorship at the University of London. This freed him to spend himself fulltime for the education of the workers.

This effort was in the short run a failure. But in a church so allied with the landed aristocracy the wonder is that it existed at all. After Maurice's death the cause was taken up

---

[41]Maurice, *The Kingdom of Christ*, ed. A.R. Vidler (London: SCM, 1958), 1.236-257; 2.237-40; 2.277-285, especially p. 284. For what follows I depend on A.M. Ramsey, *F.D. Maurice and the Conflicts of Modern Theology* (Cambridge: U.P., 1951); A. R. Vidler, *F.D. Maurice and Company* (London: SCM, 1966); Torben Christensen, *Origin and History of Christian Socialism 1848-54* (Aarhus: Universitetsforlaget, 1962).

by others, e.g., Bishop Westcott, under somewhat more favorable circumstances, and the Christian Social Union was one of the tributory streams that flowed into the Labor Party. For Maurice, the Christian's commitment to this kind of struggle for justice derived from Jesus' preaching of a divine order and a spiritual society, which Maurice called the kingdom of Christ.

As the final illustration of an understanding of the kingdom of God in this period we select the Social Gospel movement in America. Commonly dated from 1870 to 1920, its principal representatives are Washington Gladden (1836-1918), for most of his adult life a pastor in Columbus, Ohio, and Walter Rauschenbusch (1861-1918), an American Baptist pastor and professor at Colgate Seminary in Rochester, New York. We note at once that both men died during the last year of the First World War. This is symbolic. The Social Gospel movement was the theological expression of the Progressive Era in American politics. (Woodrow Wilson and the idealist philosopher Josiah Royce are other figures that bridge the two forms of concern religious and political.) It achieved much good, in moving the churches from a revivalistic concern for individual and often emotional conversion to a more collective or social awareness of human need and divine salvation, as well as in promoting some worth-while legislation, e.g., child labor laws. It also strove for better relations between churches, extending its toleration even to Roman Catholics. (Perhaps it got derailed or trivialized by becoming absorbed in the temperance movement to prohibit alcoholic beverages. Business in America was not ready for labor unions or graduated income taxes before the first World War.)

The Social Gospel movement was centered theologically in Jesus' proclamation of the kingdom of God. This is especially true in the case of Rauschenbusch, theologically the best educated of its spokesmen. He had studied in Germany and knew the thought of Ritschl and Harnack. He wrote three main books in his lifetime, but not long ago the manuscript of his first book was published. Entitled *The Righteousness of the Kingdom*, it consists of five chapters:

Christianity is Revolutionary; The Kingdom of God; The Revolutionary Power; The New Law; The New Morality. The theological heart of the book lies in the second and third chapters. The kingdom is described as a messianic theocracy for the sanctification of this life. Rauschenbusch refused to identify this kingdom only with the state, or only with the church, or only with the individual conscience though all have important parts to play in its realization. Nor does he deny a future divine act in history. (In this he differs from the continental liberals who set aside basic Christian beliefs and creeds as unmodern. Rauschenbusch, dealing with American Christians, would not have been able to make any headway had he done the same. There is no evidence that he wanted to. This marks a significant difference between Social Gospel and Ritschlian theology.) But he asks believers in a future coming this telling question: "In what does the watching [for the Son of Man] consist? In expectation or in obedience?" (p. 107). Clearly his interest lies in what *we* can do here and now, not so much in what God has done (although the Spirit of his Christ gives us the power to do what we do) or will do: "He will appear the second time when the fullness of the time shall have come. When that will be, depends largely on us" (ibid.).

That the movement could be so disillusioned by the war suggests that it had some flaws. It was doubtless too optimistic and too naive with respect to the magnitude of the problems and the chances of correction. Yet some of its most important legislative goals were achieved in the succeeding decades, and, after a time of theological chastening and deepening, it reemerged in the American churches in myriad ways, because, despite its Pelagian tendency, it was not very far off the mark, and because the need was and is so great, and because there is no completely distinct acceptable alternative.[42]

[42]R.T. Handy, ed., *The Social Gospel in America* (New York: Oxford, 1966); W. Rauschenbusch, *The Righteousness of the Kingdom* (Nashville: Abingdon, 1968); J.F. Fishburn, *The Fatherhood of God and the Victorian Family: The Social Gospel in America* (Philadelphia: Fortress, 1981), a feminist critique, and an up to

In this chapter we have surveyed a large number of authors and movements. In the Renaissance we encountered utopian visionaries like Savonarola and Campanella. In the Reformation we saw the difference between reformers allied with princes and city magistrates and reformers like the Anabaptists who were interested in a social revolution inspired by the biblical promise of the kingdom of God. Above all, we learned that it was Immanuel Kant who in his little 1793 book on religion recalled the attention of theologians and philosophers to the central hope of the synoptic gospels, the kingdom of God on earth. In practice, Kant not only interpreted the kingdom as the ethical commonwealth, but tended to assume that we build it ourselves, without the grace and gift of God. This Pelagian (we save ourselves) distortion led to both the beneficial activism and the disappointed illusions of liberal Protestantism and the Social Gospel movement in the nineteenth century. In a quieter vein movements were afoot in Social Catholicism which led to various workers' organizations and a series of social encyclicals. The stage was set for the rediscovery and appropriation of the eschatological nature of the kingdom.

date guide to research. Cf. Donald Meyer, *The Protestant Search for Political Realism 1919-1941* (Berkeley: University of California, 1960), p. 285: "The final upshot of the social gospel was that the gospel had to become more personal." The classic survey for the colonial period and the nineteenth century is H.R. Niebuhr, *The Kingdom of God in America* (New York: Harper, 1937).

5. THE KINGDOM OF GOD IN TWENTIETH-CENTURY THOUGHT

In this chapter we intend to trace the recovery or retrieval of the original eschatological kingdom proclamation of Jesus, the resistances to this rediscovery, and its growing influence in the present century. The issue is not so much exegetical, although there are some lingering problems in this area too, as it is theological and practical. For there is a sense in which scholars always knew of the eschatological-apocalyptic aspect of the kingdom concept but they hesitated to take it seriously and for a variety of reasons. Was not the hope of its coming proven false by the delay of the Parousia? Is it not too mythological-fanciful-utopian for a modern Christian believer to take seriously? Is it not useless from the viewpoint of practical ethics, since, if you think God will bring it suddenly, you do not need to do anything about it yourself? Does it not conflict with other perceptions of salvation in Christ, like justification by faith alone? Is it not "too Jewish" for Gentile Christians? Is it not intrinsically impossible, since our finite world of space and time is incapable of receiving such a massive inbreaking of the divine infinite perfection? Would a world without gross injustice and warfare not be insufferably boring, or worse, tyrannically oppressive? Does not freedom mean also freedom for criminals—at least of the genteel sort? Was the historical Jesus really interested in social, political and economic transformation?

These are, some of them at least, serious questions. They are questions with which twentieth century theologians have wrestled. Some of their answers will appear in the story of the understanding of the kingdom of God as it unfolds here. This part of the story has been told several times before, and well, in English.[1] Therefore we can be briefer about it until we come to the most recent developments, which have not yet been chronicled in a historical survey.

We begin with Johannes Weiss and his little bombshell. He was born in 1863, the son of a noted New Testament scholar, Bernhard Weiss, and the son-in-law of Albrecht Ritschl. He died suddenly at fifty-one, as professor in Heidelberg, in 1914. As a member of the history-of-religions school of New Testament studies, he was interested in the highest degree of historical honesty, in understanding the

---

[1]Gösta Lundström, *The Kingdom of God in the Teaching of Jesus: A History of Interpretation from the Last Decades of the Nineteenth Century to the Present Day* (Edinburgh: Oliver and Boyd, 1963; Swedish orig. 1947) devotes some space to the philosophical and systematic theological contributions to the discussion. Norman Perrin, *The Kingdom of God in the Teaching of Jesus* (Philadelphia: Westminster, 1963), is the classic survey whose conclusions seem to us balanced and correct, unlike his later waverings between historical and literary-metaphorical understandings in *Jesus and the Language of the Kingdom* (Philadelphia: Fortress, 1976). Cf. his SBL presidential address "Eschatology and Hermeneutics: Reflections on Method in the Interpretation of the New Testament," *JBL* 93 (1974) 3-14; "The Interpretation of a Biblical Symbol," *JR* 55 (1975) 348-370. A fascinating and frank report from Germany comes from Klaus Koch, *The Rediscovery of Apocalyptic* (SBT, n.s. 22; Naperville: Allenson, 1972). He is particularly good on German resistance to apocalyptic, pointing out that all German commentaries on Daniel in this century were written by non-Germans (Bentzen, Porteous, Ringgren). He notes the curious fact that eschatology and revelation are positive terms in the German theological vocabulary but that apocalyptic (which means revelatory in Greek) has a negative connotation. He also documents the two escape-hatches commonly used to evade the apocalyptic dimension of Jesus' message: (1) the Old Testament scholar's theory of the "prophetic connection" between Jesus and Second Isaiah, which skips the exile, Ezra and Daniel; (2) the New Testament scholar's theory of the non-apocalyptic Jesus and his apocalyptic church. These are "the agonised attempts to save Jesus from apocalyptic" (p. 57). These debates continue to go on. Cf. the comically entitled exchange in *NTS*: Ragnar Leivestad, "Exit the Apocalyptic Son of Man," 18 (1971) 243-267; Barnabas Lindars," Re-Enter the Apocalyptic Son of man," 22 (1975) 52-72.

Scriptures as rooted in their time and place, even when this meant presenting early Christianity as strange, foreign, distant, "unmodern." He applied this approach which we may summarize as "seek the historical truth and let the theological-pastoral chips fall where they may" to the eschatology of the synoptic gospels in 1892, in a sixty-seven page brochure called *Jesus' Proclamation of the Kingdom of God.*.[2]

Exegetically Weiss came to conclusions similar to those which we have presented in chapter one. In contrast with the neo-Kantian problematic of his father-in-law he concluded: "The Kingdom of God as Jesus thought of it is never something subjective, inward, or spiritual, but is always the objective messianic Kingdom, which usually is pictured as a territory into which one enters, or as a land in which one has a share, or as a treasure which comes down from heaven."[3] It was the end of Kant's Pelagian "ethical commonwealth" which we build on our own.

Weiss' work provoked a firestorm of criticism. He replied with a new, expanded, more restrained edition of his work, and then, with another little book tracing the history of the idea, he tried to calm the outrage down by suggesting that, while his view was historically true, it might be viewed as pastorally useless and theologically imprudent. He would rest content if his historical conclusions were conceded to be sound. By beating a tactical retreat to an academic ivory tower, he won time for his view to be more carefully considered. But, of course, once he had unleashed his bolt, things could never be the same for theologians who took Christianity seriously as a historically grounded faith. Theologians could only proceed with integrity if they could refute the historical basis of Weiss' judgment or else assimilate his historical judgment as correct and adjust their theology accordingly. Roughly speaking, we could say that it took

---

[2]Göttingen: Vandenhoeck & Ruprecht. Translated by R.H. Hiers and D.L. Holland (Philadelphia: Fortress, 1971). Cf. Rolf Schäfer, "Das Reich Gottes bei Albrecht Ritschl und Johannes Weiss," *Z TK* 61 (1964) 68-88.

[3]Eng. trans., p. 133.

Weiss' view fifty years to conquer the exegetical world and another twenty or so to make a serious impact on systematic theology (assuming that this would date from Moltmann's *Theology of Hope* whose first edition appeared in 1964).

But, even as Weiss retired from the field, a brash champion of his views entered the lists. In 1906, the gifted thirty-one year old musician, philosopher, theologian and future jungle-doctor Albert Schweitzer published a survey of nineteenth century lives of Jesus, "*From Reimarus to Wrede.*"[4] If a violent metaphor be allowed, we could say that in this lengthy review Schweitzer used Weiss' original little book as a razor with which to slit the throats of all his predecessors. To put it less violently, he used Weiss as a measuring rod of historical accuracy. By this standard they almost all fell short. Against them Schweitzer wished to make two points. The so-called historical Jesus of the nineteenth century biographies is really a modernization, in which Jesus is painted in the colors of modern bourgeois respectability and neo-Kantian moralism. Secondly, the real Jesus of Nazareth was actually less "modern" than the Nicene Christ, because he was the high watermark of Jewish apocalypticism. This second point, with its Christological reference, points to a difference of interest between Weiss and Schweitzer, who are usually presented as holding identical views. This is true for the point crucial to our focus, the understanding of Jesus' teaching on the kingdom. But Weiss largely confined himself to the reconstruction of Jesus' *teaching*, which had a good chance to be achieved successfully. Schweitzer more boldly attempted to construct an entire life of Jesus, including a Christology. This ambitious project could not be carried off so easily and left him open to charges that his reconstructed Jesus was not truer than the others, only uglier. Schweitzer's Jesus is indeed ugly if the viewer is an anti-Semite or uninterested in social justice, because he is both Jewish and apocalyptic. Schweitzer's Christological focus unfortunately

---

[4]Translated by William Montgomery as *The Quest of the Historical Jesus* (New York: Macmillan, 1910).

got side-tracked in a protracted debate on whether Jesus had made an error in timing. Did Jesus teach that the kingdom would come in the lifetime of his immediate followers? Cf. Mark 9:1; 13:30; Matt 10:23; but also Mark 13:32-35. This concern about Jesus' perfect knowledge, about the delay of the coming, about timing, proved a distraction, but not before it had disturbed consciences. Eventually a banal consensus formed that Jesus had expected the kingdom to come soon, but without calculating or predicting exact times. The interim for which he allowed could be understood today as having turned into an outright error, or, conversely, as still imposing on believers a dynamic, energizing eschatological urgency. For those for whom Jesus' message is still significant, the second alternative is obviously preferable.[5]

In retrospect, we can see that Schweitzer's significance in the kingdom story consists above all in his promotion of Weiss' apocalyptic breakthrough. He did this by relating Weiss' work to the Jesus studies of the previous century and by extending its implications into the study of Paul, and beyond biblical studies into a coherent religions philosophy (strongly influenced by Kant, it must be admitted). By his long life, full of intellectual and humanitarian labors, lavishly covered by the media, and ultimately crowned by the Nobel peace prize, he did more to make Weiss' work known and loved than any other single person, and more than compensated for Weiss' early death.[6]

The theologians took time out from the eschatological debate during the First World War. In the twenties there were many adjustments. The old liberals tried to parallel the

---

[5]Landmarks in the consensus were Oscar Cullmann's *Christ and Time* (Philadelphia: Westminster, 1964; orig. 1946), and W.G. Kümmel's *Promise and Fulfillment* (SBT 23; Naperville: Allenson, 1961). R. Schnackenburg was still fretting apologetically about the *scientia Christi* problem in 1959, *God's Rule and Kingdom* (New York: Herder, 1963), pp. 203-214.

[6]Schweitzer had two Swiss professional disciples who attempted to carry his consistent or thoroughgoing eschatology into the history of doctrine and systematics but without finding the right key: Martin Werner, *The Formation of Christian Dogma* (New York: Harper, 1957). Fritz Buri, *Die Bedeutung der neutestamentlichen Eschatologie für die neuere protestantische Theologie* (Zurich: EVB, 1934).

noble Kantian idealism of the League of Nations with corresponding efforts at ecclesial collaboration and ecumenism. This they undertook through two organizations, *Faith and Order*, and *Life and Work*, the forerunners of the World Council of Churches. Alongside these international efforts there were other, more sharply focused, gatherings. One of these was a conference of twelve German and English theologians on the kingdom of God, held at the deanery of Canterbury in 1927, under the chairmanship of G.K.A. Bell. Every effort at balance was made and biblical, historical and systematic aspects were covered. In retrospect, most of the papers are not very satisfactory, but two are important still. In planning the biblical papers, the organizers took for granted that there was an "other-worldly kingdom" and a "this-worldly kingdom." This distinction is of questionable utility, but C.H. Dodd and Gerhard Kittel had little difficulty exchanging harmless pleasantries on the this-worldly kingdom. The real battle occurred on the other-worldly kingdom. Here Karl Ludwig Schmidt presented the full, pure Weissian doctrine: the kingdom comes to earth from the transcendent God, accompanied by a cosmic "castastrophe," as a free, future divine miracle. Sir Edwyn Hoskyns, by contrast, offered a remarkably frank and clearheaded statement of the Anglican position. He said that for Paul (2 Cor 3), Luke-Acts, and John, Christianity was primarily a possession (of the Holy Spirit, justification, the new creation, etc.) and only consequently and secondarily a hope. For Luke "the coming of the Spirit is the true eschatology, the end, the new order of God, and, consequently he means his readers to understand, since Pentecost all true converts stand within the kingdom of God." Hoskyns then goes on to take his major stand on John:

> The eschatological sayings of Jesus, which in the earlier Gospels appeared to contemplate the end of the world, are ... in the Johannine writings, simply and consciously, transformed into prophecies of the coming of the Spirit which was to follow the death and resurrection of the Son of God.

This transformation was the great triumph of primitive Christian thought, and emerged as a result of reflection upon the traditional words of Jesus in the light of Christian faith and experience. Christianity was thereby transformed from a small company of men and women who expected the end of the world to be imminent into the Catholic Religion of men and women who had found God, and entered into the sphere of righteousness and truth. With the compositon of the Lukan and Johannine writings Christianity may be said to have found its feet, and the writers were in a position to contemplate a future history, though in fact they never actually do so.

The question may be raised at this point whether the Pauline-Lukan-Johannine interpretation of our Lord's teaching was really justifiable. Was the triumph of Christian reflection a triumph at the expense of His plain teaching? If once it be granted that His teaching and actions were throughout mainly symbolical, the eschatological language may also be treated as imagery adequate to express His conviction that the advent of the kingdom would not merely follow, but would be inaugurated by His death. To speak humanly He knew Himself to be standing on the brink of a new spiritual order, which would fulfill the longings of the greatest of the Hebrew prophets. The traditional eschatological imagery provided him with a vehicle to express the significance of His life and death. If this be regarded as in any way a probable view, the Johannine writings may well be treated as the first completely satisfactory interpretation of His teaching.[7]

This plain statement requires a few comments. First, exegetically, Paul and Luke retain more of Jesus' future eschatology than Hoskyns allows, and even John is not so closed or one-sidedly present oriented as Hoskyns seems to

---

[7]The papers of the conference are published in *Theology* 14 (1927) 247-295. The Hoskyns citation is from p. 252f. R.H. Fuller has memorialized Hoskyns in *NTS* 30 (1984) 321-334, "Sir Edwyn Hoskyns and the Contemporary Relevance of Biblical Theology," cf. esp. pp. 332f.

think. Apart from John 14:3 ("I will come again"), it remains true for John that "the hour is coming," even though "it now is" (4:23; 5:25). Secondly, the "triumph" of a purely realized eschatology would indeed be at the expense of Jesus' "plain teaching." To be sure, one can, with Bultmann, hold that the teaching of Jesus does not belong to the content of Christian theology. But if one finds meaning in Jesus' eschatological promise, in his hope-filled future orientation, then one will be reluctant, even as an alert, contemporary, critical Christian, to dispense so lightly with his kingdom message. With respect to the question of imagery, symbol and metaphor, let it suffice to say that Jesus did indeed speak in parables, but not only in parables. The parables must be interpreted in the light of his aphorisms. Moreover, he spoke of the things of God, of which the kingdom is one, and divine matters must always be mysterious to men. But Jesus gives the mystery some intelligible content, namely, that it involves a future divine act on earth which brings in its train a fullness of justice and peace. How that will happen can be spoken only in figures. But the figures point to something definite, not to the void.

It is to be noted that Hoskyns conceded that the earlier gospels were apocalyptic. He simply proposed to ignore them. On the Continent other ways of facing the eschatological challenge had already emerged. Karl Barth had broken with Harnack in his *The Epistle to the Romans*.[8] This is very likely the most important single work of twentieth century theology and created a new era. To describe this new era is not so easy. Barth fused an amalgam of Paul, Reformation theology, Kierkegaard, Dostoievsky, Nietzsche and his own pastoral experience into a rejection of the old Kantian liberal moralism and, more important, a recapturing of revelation as God actually speaking through the biblical text as a power of God unto salvation, as descending "vertically from above." This shift had both

[8]First edition 1919; second 1922. English version by E.C. Hoskyns, Oxford: University Press, 1933.

positive and negative effects. Negatively, it could develop into a woolly, existentialist decisionism that could remain limited to the individual believer, a mere represtination of the past and compatible with National Socialism (e.g., F. Gogarten). Positively, it meant a revitalization of basic Christian faith whch could stand up to the challenges of the Hitler era. Thus Barth himself helped some German Protestant churchmen to take their courageous stand in the Barmen Declaration of 1934 against Nazi totalitarian claims and racist ideology.[9] This cost him his German professorship. One of his finest Lutheran protégés, Dietrich Bonhoeffer, derived from Barth the courage to renew the ethics of the Sermon on the Mount as the cost of discipleship and against all "cheap grace." Bonhoeffer went on to advise the conspirators who attempted to assassinate Hitler on 20 July 1944. He and they paid for this with their lives.

Barth admitted that the New Testament message was eschatological: "If Christianity be not altogether thoroughgoing eschatology, there remains in it no relationship whatever with Christ" (*Romans*, p. 314). But he interpreted this away in an existential way. He did not, at least in his dialectical phase, make the kingdom a central focus of his theology or admit that it was apocalyptic. The most positive contribution that Barth made to the recovery of the kingdom of God theme in theology is that by restoring the dogmatic tradition of the church in revelation, Trinitology, Christology and soteriology he created a climate more open to biblical eschatology and biblical theology in general. It remained for Barthians of the next generation to unite a high Christology and Trinitology with a conviction of the truth and value of the kingdom of God theme, thereby correcting the errors of the nineteenth century secular, Pelagian understanding of it.

Let us now look at some of the great exegetes of the thirties and forties. Rudolf Bultmann, for a time associated

[9]Arthur Cochrane, *The Church's Confession Under Hitler* (Philadelphia: Westminster, 1962); Peter Matheson, *The Third Reich and the Christian Churches* (Grand Rapids: Eerdmans, 1981).

with Barth, carried the existentialist line further in the direction of a thorough-going demythologizing of all biblical concepts that taxed the imagination or the reason. As an acute historian he could see that Jesus was an apocalypticist, but he rejected Jesus' teaching as having any direct bearing on Christian theology. "The message of Jesus belongs to the presupposition of the theology of the New Testament and is not a part of that theology itself."[10] Once Jesus' message is safely confined to the dustbin of history Bultmann could be very clear about it.

> The dominant concept of Jesus' message is the Reign of God. Jesus proclaims its immediately impending irruption, now already making itself felt. Reign of God is an eschatological concept. It means the regime of God which will destroy the present course of the world, wipe out all the contra-divine, Satanic power under which the present world groans—and thereby, terminating all pain and sorrow, bring in salvation for the People of God which awaits the fulfillment of the prophets' promises. The coming of God's Reign is a miraculous event, which will be brought about by God alone without the help of men.[11]

This definition is historically accurate, but for Bultmann it is also theologically false. What we see here is a chasm between history and theology.

The great British exegete Charles Harold Dodd shared a common goal with Bultmann. Both men felt a mission to recommend the Christian faith to their university colleagues. They thought that the best way to do this was through the Fourth Gospel and to its interpretation therefore they devoted their best efforts. But Dodd was reluctant to abandon the Synoptic Gospels to the ash-heap of history lest his interpretation of John be itself thereby undercut. To

---

[10]R. Bultmann, *Theology of the New Testament* (New York: Scribner's, 1951), 1.3 retranslated more literally.

[11]Bultmann, *Theology*, p. 4.

show that John's was not an eccentric interpretation of Jesus, he felt obliged to show already in the synoptics what he called a "realized eschatology," that is, that already in the ministry of the historical Jesus the kingdom was present in its fullness. This difficult task he thought he could accomplish through the parables. Thus, in his *The Parables of the Kingdom* of 1935,[12] he endeavored to prove that the Lord's Prayer refers to the past and present, not to the future.

> The Church prays, "Thy Kingdom come." As it prays, it remembers that the Lord did come, and with Him came the Kingdom of God. Uniting memory with aspiration, it discovers that He comes. He comes in His Cross and Passion; He comes in the glory of His Father with the holy angels. Each communion is not a stage in a process by which His coming draws gradually nearer, or a milestone on the road by which we slowly approach the distant goal of the Kingdom of God on earth. It is a re-living of the decisive moment at which He came. The preaching of the Church is directed towards reconstituting in the experience of individuals the hour of decision which Jesus brought.[13]

This is elegantly moving but exegetically unpersuasive, taking the words exactly contrary to their plain sense. Dodd's great contemporary Joachim Jeremias made short work of his "realized eschatology."

Joachim Jeremias, whose special strength lies in his mastery of Aramaic and early rabbinic literature, corrected Dodd's "contraction of eschatology" by his own formulation "a self-realizing eschatology," which has also been translated as "an eschatology in process of realization." He interprets the parables of growth as teaching not about the process itself but about the suddenness with which the kingdom will come; for example, in the parable of the mustard seed (Mark

---

[12]London: Nisbet, 1935; rev. ed. 1961.
[13]Dodd, *Parables*, p. 152.

4:30-32), "when it is sown it grows up and becomes the greatest of all shrubs."[14] When Jeremias comes to state his summary understanding of the proclamation of Jesus, his treatment of the kingdom is close to the Weissian line: "the basileia is always and everywhere understood in eschatological terms; it denotes the time of salvation, the consummation of the world, the restoration of the disrupted communion between God and man. . . Its chief characteristic is that God is realizing the ideal of the king of righteousness."[15] Unlike Bultmann, Jeremias believes this message is part of the theology of the New Testament.

At this point in our narrative we consider how the Weissian view began to break out of existentialist shackles and to spread into new regions. Oscar Cullmann acted as a bridge between Protestants and Catholics, between German and French cultures, because his books were always published in German and French, and because for years he taught one semester in Basel and one semester in Paris. As an Alsatian he was perfectly bilingual. His *Christ and Time* (1946) had an enormous influence in both cultures, both confessions, and affected systematic theologians, philosophers of history and historians of religion (e.g., Daniélou, Eliade, Löwith). Curiously his Basel colleague Karl Barth so disagreed with him on the point of eschatology that he is reported to have once said, in good Dodge City fashion, "Basel is not big enough for the two of us."

After the Second World War Roman Catholic exegesis began to regain its sea legs, energized by the needs of the times and by papal encouragement. Two exegetes attempted major efforts in the biblical theology of the kingdom. Joseph Bonsirven, S.J., an expert in early rabbinics, did well with the Old Testament and Jewish background, but interpreted the gospels in the direction of Bergsonian evolutionary progressivism and Kantian moralism, turning the kingdom

---

[14]Jeremias, *The Parables of Jesus* (New York: Scribner's, 1963), pp. 21, 229.

[15]Jeremias, *New Testament Theology* (New York: Scribner's, 1971), pp. 96-108, esp. p. 102.

theme into a treatise on ethics.[16] It was left to Rudolf Schnackenburg, of Würzburg, to write the great Catholic book on the subject, *God's Rule and Kingdom* (1959).[17] Perrin judges it "probably the best discussion of the subject."[18] Why does he say that? Perhaps because Schnackenburg exhibits the virtue of thoroughness. He treats every relevant text from the Old Testament, Judaism, and the *entire* New Testament. By casting his net so widely he cannot fail to turn up some useful fresh material. But his book finds its unity in the focus on Christ and the religious meaning of the kingdom. To summarize, Schnackenburg has taken a major step forward for Catholics. He is the first to break definitively with Augustine's identification of the kingdom on earth as the church. Balancing this positive step, there is a negative one. For Schnackenburg, "the salvation proclaimed and promised by Jesus in this reign . . . is purely religious in character. Jesus entirely excluded the national and the politico-religious elements from his *basileia* concept."[19] This spiritualizing interpretation is understandable in the light of European political experience in the recent past and historically correct to the extent that Jesus was not a narrow nationalist. He proclaimed a universal kingdom. But that universal kingdom does have social political consequences.

Meanwhile a change was occurring among the disciples of Bultmann. The most brilliant and independent of them, Ernst Käsemann (b. 1906), shocked his confreres in 1953 with a paper on the problem of the historical Jesus.[20] This inaugurated the so-called "new quest" of the historical Jesus but, more important for us, it made the point that Christian theology could not ignore the teaching of Jesus. (For one thing, the theological students would no longer tolerate this

[16] J. Bonsirven, *Le Régne de Dieu* (Paris: Aubier, 1957).

[17] The English translation by John Murray appeared in 1963 (New York: Herder & Herder).

[18] Perrin, *Jesus and the Language of the Kingdom*, p. 210.

[19] *God's Rule*, p. 95.

[20] *Essays on New Testament Themes* (Naperville: Allenson, 1964), pp. 15–47.

neglect.) The consequence of this was obvious: since Jesus' teaching was heavily eschatological, Christian theology had to come to terms with his apocalyptic. Sure enough, in 1960 Käsemann followed up his first essay with another, "The Beginnings of Christian Theology," which had as its key thesis that "apocalyptic was the mother of all Christian theology."[21] This was greeted with enough dismay and outrage for him to follow it up with another "On the Subject of Primitive Christian Apocalyptic."[22] Some of the details of Käsemann's reconstruction of Jesus' teaching as that of a liberal Lutheran and his ascribing apocalyptic to the "post-Easter enthusiasm" of the church are more than a little doubtful. But his main points, that Christian theology begins apocalyptic, and that Paul himself shares this outlook, have withstood criticism and influenced the next generation of exegetes and systematicians.[23]

The final part of our survey is devoted to the growing influence of the kingdom theme on systematic theology and on contemporary religio-political events. We must step back for a moment to notice three major figures on the American scene who represent a non-apocalyptic understanding of the kingdom, Paul Tillich, Reinhold Niebuhr, and Langdon Gilkey. Tillich was of course born in Germany and was steeped in the culture of his country and engaged in its struggles. In a futile effort to stem the tide of fascism, he joined a little group of Religious Socialists and wrote a book called *The Socialist Decision*.[24] The book came out two

[21] *New Testament Questions of Today* (London: SCM, 1969), pp. 82-107, citation on p. 102.

[22] *New Testament Questions*, pp. 108-137. This essay was replying to his early critics Ebeling and Fuchs. Bultmann himself weighed in later with an essay entitled "Ist die Apokalyptik die Mutter der christlichen Theologie?" reprinted in his *Exegetica* (Tübingen: Mohr, 1967), pp. 476-482.

[23] Regarding Paul, Käsemann has pursued his line of interpretation both in essays and in his fine commentary on Romans. This approach has been systematized by J.C. Beker, *Paul the Apostle* (Philadelphia: Fortress, 1980), in what amounts to a kind of Käsemannian scholasticism, whose apocalyptic emphasis remains basically sound and an advance over previous studies.

[24] (New York: Harper, 1977).

months after the Nazi seizure of power. It cost him his chair and his future in his own country. In exile in America he had, for a long time, to avoid political matters. The war and the McCarthy era were not opportune moments for a foreigner to meddle in such things. But, as he won greater acceptance in the United States and as he came to the third and final volume of his *Systematic Theology* (1963),[25] he returned to his old socio-political concerns. There, in the last major part of the system, he treats "history and the kingdom of God" (pp. 297-423).

In the early work Tillich had criticized fascism as a myth of origins on the basis of Christianity as a myth (or revelation) of eschatological expectation. In his final statement he has included all manner of interesting reflections (e.g., on the Christian meaning of the great Western empires, p. 340), but for our purposes two aspects need be noted.

What is the kingdom of God for Tillich? He classifies it as a comprehensive religious symbol. Its inner-historical side is manifest through the Spiritual Presence. Its transhistorical side is identical with Eternal Life. It has four characteristics: it is political, social, personalistic, and universal. This is a useful list and true as far as it goes. The justice and peace dimensions are clear in his explanations. But it omits the explicitly religious, spiritual or divine dimension, even though this is present in the context. This weakness has been corrected by Edward Schillebeeckx. In his long work *Christ* (1980), Schillebeeckx takes up Tillich's list and adds three more components of which the most important in this connection is "humanity's utopian religious consciousness" or awareness of God.[26]

Tillich's kingdom then has affinities with the spiritual-mystical and ecclesial types we have seen in the Fathers. He is close in spirit to Augustine. On earth we only have momentary, fragmentary anticipations of salvation. And eternal life lies beyond history. There is no expectation of a further divine act bringing eternity into time.

[25](Chicago: University of Chicago, 1963), pp. 356-54.
[26](New York: Seabury, 1980), pp. 731-743.

Reinhold Niebuhr comes to similar conclusions but by a different path. Missouri-born, he was more a practical than a philosophical theologian. His influence on American church and social policy has been considerable. His task in his first major book, *Moral Man and Immoral Society* (1932),[27] was to overcome the blunders of the old Social Gospel theology. He reminded his readers of the depths of human sinfulness, the magnitude and systemic nature of social evils. He explained that private morality and good intentions were inadequate to deal with the problems. Naive assumptions concerning the inevitability of progress and the essential goodness of humanity must go. At the time Niebuhr expressed admiration for the German Center party as a model of Christian social action, but its subsequent failure to stop Hitler later disenchanted him. Niebuhr's theology might have led him to apathetic resignation but in fact it did not.

The Social Gospel leaders had composed a "social creed of the churches" and it was adopted by the then Federal Council of the Churches of Christ in America in 1908. It advocated abolition of child labor, better working conditions for women, one day off during the week, and the right of every worker to a living wage. But it did not include the right to unionize. Niebuhr had worked as a pastor in Detroit, had let the union organizers meet in the church hall, and had helped overcome the opposition of Henry Ford. His influence led the successor National Council of Churches to support the right to unionize and contributed to the formulation of New Deal legislation in the 1930's. His theology helped to shape not only pastors but also government officials.[28]

Because the Social Gospel had placed such emphasis on building the kingdom here and now ourselves, Niebuhr felt obliged by his "Christian realism" to avoid building his theology of social justice on this theme. For him the kingdom of God is beyond history. A few years before he

[27](New York: Scribner's, 1932).

[28]Catholics too were active in the labor movement and in building support for the New Deal, especially Monsignor John A. Ryan, known as Right Reverend New Dealer.

died, he met one of the young German kingdom theologians, Wolfhart Pannenberg. When talk turned to the kingdom he warned: "Social thought that begins with the kingdom of God, or even emphasizes it very much, inevitably ends up with utopianism. We've been through this business of the kingdom before."[29]

Langdon Gilkey was a student of both Tillich and Niebuhr. He has remained faithful to their heritage which stands in the Augustinian line. He dedicates his major work on our topic to them: *Reaping the Whirlwind: A Christian Interpretation of History* (1976).[30] In this work he builds on neo-orthodox historical pessimism but he goes far beyond it in the direction of secularist despair - despite all his talk of hope. Not only is the world incorrigibly evil but now, in the view of process theology, God is too weak to do anything but set forth the kingdom as a "lure" for humanity which is destined ever to seek it but never to attain it. In this perspective, "the characteristics of the kingdom ... are life, community and love, or, to bring these closer to political norms: being, participation, and responsible concern."[31]

The New Era

The dawn of a new era in theology and faith requires a new stimulus. Exegesis had made its apocalyptic point with Weiss and Schweitzer. Barth had revived confidence in the Bible as God's revelation. Marxist revolution posed an external threat and challenge. Death-of-God "theology" provided an alarm signal from within the Christian community. These elements were then fused into an ultimate challenge to theologians by Ernst Bloch in his *The Principle Hope*.[32] Bloch (1885-1977) is a very unusual combination of

---

[29]Related by R.J. Neuhaus in his introduction to W. Pannenberg, *Theology and the Kingdom of God* (Philadelphia: Westminster, 1969), p. 32.

[30](New York: Seabury, 1976).

[31]*Reaping the Whirlwind*, pp. 288-291.

[32]A selection has been given in *Man on His Own* (New York: Herder, 1970). Complete translation, Cambridge, Mass.: M.I.T. Press, 1986.

elements: a Jewish atheist Marxist philosopher of religion, too religious for East German Communists, too Marxist for most Westerners. His work is a remarkable interpretation of many of the religious traditions of Western civilization, and especially of the Bible, an interpretation which finds in these sources the voices of the oppressed of every age crying for liberation. Although one cannot help wondering at times whether his professed atheism is only a pose, the stated intent of his work is to retrieve the truth of the religious traditions for an age without any god but man. His mastery of the tradition is so great and his reinterpretations so clever and provocative, that any theologian who takes him seriously and yet cannot, with the best will in the world, believe that man is god, feels compelled to respond to the challenge he represents and this in a way different from the challenge represented by Marx. Marx did not write as a professional theologian or discuss the religious tradition in its details. Bloch does. He brings the Marxist option directly into the center of theological discussion. For Bloch religions are the guardians of hope, especially of eschatological, messianic hope. And Christianity is the anticipation of the kingdom of absolute freedom.

Theologians were quick to take up Bloch's gauntlet. Among them doubtless the most important is Jürgen Moltmann (b. 1926), professor in Tübingen. His *Theology of Hope* appeared in 1964 and was translated in 1967, at a time when believers were dismayed by "death-of-God" theology and the real death of John F. Kennedy. It is not surprising that the work was received enthusiastically. But Moltmann had deep roots in the Calvinist side of German Protestantism, one may say, and attempted to advance the Barthian biblical theology movement into a new era by fusing neo-orthodoxy with biblical eschatology as a theological answer to Bloch and, more importantly, as a Christian message to the aspirations of the struggling peoples of the world. In the light of the Exodus experience of Israel and of the risen Christ Moltmann wrestles with biblical eschatology and modern philosophies of history and tradition. By taking seriously the biblical promises for the future (on earth and not only in heaven) Moltmann attempts to move the churches out of their rut wherein they look only to past saving events. He tries to turn their attention to the future promised by God, of which Exodus and Easter are a foretaste. He also strives to overcome Bultmann's existential and individualistic decisionism by pointing out the universal and cosmic dimensions of salvation.

Moltmann's work is the theological highpoint of the story we are telling. It would serve no useful purpose to try to summarize his entire thought. Page after page is quotable as a balanced, nuanced theological affirmation of the implications of future, this worldly, divinely realized eschatology. Moltmann twice treats of the kingdom *ex professo*. We will merely select one citation from each kingdom section.

> If the promise of the kingdom of God shows us a universal eschatological future horizon spanning all things ... then it is impossible for the man of hope to adopt an attitude of religious and cultic resignation from the world. On the contrary, he is compelled to accept the world in all meekness, subject as it is to death and the powers of annihilation, and to guide all things towards their new being ... He becomes rightless with the rightless, for the sake of the divine right that is coming.[33]
>
> The goal of the Christian mission ... aims at reconciliation with God, at forgiveness of sins and abolition of godlessness. But salvation must also be understood as *shalom* in the Old Testament sense. This does not mean merely salvation of the soul, individual rescue from the evil world, comfort for the troubled conscience, but also the realization of the eschatological *hope of justice*, *humanizing* of man, the *socializing* of humanity, *peace* for all creation.[34]

Moltmann has carried this program through in subsequent

---

[33] *Theology of Hope: On the Ground and Implications of a Christian Eschatology* (New York: Harper, 1967), p. 224; cf. pp. 216-224.

[34] *Theology of Hope*, p. 329; cf. pp. 325-9.

works, *The Crucified God*, *The Church in the Power of the Spirit*, and has returned explicitly to our theme in *Trinity and Kingdom of God*, to mention only the major stages.

The futurist orientation in theology is carried forward by many of Moltmann's colleagues in Germany and America, notably by Wolfhart Pannenberg. The latter's little *Theology and the Kingdom of God*[35] remains an excellent introduction to this way of thinking. It lays stress on the *provisionality* of all social structures until the future fulfillment, including the structures of the church. Johannes Baptist Metz, who began as Karl Rahner's assistant, has broken with him on eschatology and developed a Catholic form of this teaching in his *Theology of the World*[36] and *Followers of Christ*.[37] Metz builds on Augustine's *memoria passionis* (recalling of the suffering of Christ) as a power energizing for the future and he reaffirms the legitimacy and necessity of faith in and proclamation of the *parousia:* "Hope does not spring out of the unknown nor impel us into what is accidental. It has its roots in Christ, and even among us Christians of the late twentieth century it demands the expectation of his second coming."[38]

These European spiritual leaders have American representatives, Lutherans like Carl Braaten,[39] Reformed like Douglas Meeks, Catholic like Francis Schüssler Fiorenza,[40] who attempt to relate this emphasis to their own faith traditions and to the American experience.

While this genteel or paleface theological sea change was taking place north of the equator, the Christian sleeping giant of Latin America was waking to historical-spiritual

[35](Philadelphia: Westminster, 1969).

[36](New York: Herder & Herder, 1969).

[37](New York: Paulist, 1978).

[38]*Followers of Christ*, p. 83. Metz finds continuing meaning in vowed religious life as a kind of "shock therapy" for lukewarm Christianity insofar as this life points to God's radical future.

[39]*The Future of God: The Revolutionary Dynamics of Hope* (New York: Harper, 1969).

[40]"Dialectical Theology and Hope," *Heythrop Journal* 9/10 (1968/9), in four parts; "'Political Theology'": an historical analysis,' *Theology Digest* 25 (1977) 317-334.

consciousness. This awakening expressed itself in a flood of publications collectively described as the theology of liberation, some of them authored by real redskins. Unlike earlier Latin efforts, these publications have often received translation and critical attention in Europe and North America. As in any large movement, the quality of reflection varies and there are regional variations, e.g., Brazilian theologians are sometimes gentler than Spanish-speaking ones, it is said.

There can be no question here of an exhaustive account of recent Latin American theology. The new movement is commonly dated from the Latin American bishops' conference at Medellín, Columbia, in 1968. The meeting's purpose was to apply the church reforms of Vatican II to the Latin American situation. The first major theological expression, *A Theology of Liberation*,[41] came from the pen of a Peruvian Indian priest, Gustavo Gutierrez. As a sample of his kingdom theology we may cite from a recent lecture he gave at Harvard:

> The central point of the message of Jesus is ... the kingdom of God, the kingdom of life, peace, justice, freedom. Our God, the God of Jesus Christ, is the God of the kingdom. All attempts to separate God from the kingdom are idolatry, that is to say, to worship and to serve a false God. The kingdom is the expression of the will of God for our lives. It is the final meaning of human history. The kingdom is the always new and uncomfortable eruption of God in our lives. One permanent temptation for Christians ... is to pray the Our Father in this way: "Our Father, who art in heaven, remain there." Idolatry is this: idolatry is to separate God from the kingdom.[42]

[41](Maryknoll: Orbis, 1973).

[42]*Harvard Divinity Bulletin*, June-August 1984, p. 4. For documentation on those who would separate God from his kingdom, see the hard-hitting article by the lay historian Enrique Dussel, "The Kingdom of God and the Poor," *International Review of Missions* 68 (1979), no. 270, pp. 115-130.

Gutierrez had earlier spoken eloquently about how, while in Europe they debate the death of theology, in Latin America they talk about the death of the theologian. Since 1968 over two hundred priests and theologians have lost their lives violently after publicly opting for the poor. This is an important aspect of Latin American theology. This theology is so immediately involved in direct practice in an often critically urgent situation that it frightens armchair theologians. This is especially the case when it takes on an overtly Marxist character, as it does in the learned Mexican exegete José Porfirio Miranda.[43]

Resistance to this Marxist tendency has not been slow in coming. Liberation theology merits the distinction of being probably the first theology especially investigated by a U.S. congressional committee (sponsored by Senator Jeremiah Denton, Republican of Alabama). Of course this investigation was more interested in the morale and motivation of Central American guerrillas than in the fine points of theology. The British Broadcasting Corporation sponsored a radio lecture series against this theology delivered by E.R. Norman. Norman took loose statements from Third World bishops' pastorals and denounced them, rather than tackling the nuanced thought of the professional theologians.

It is obvious that this account is taking us to today's headlines. Most recently the Vatican's highest doctrinal authority after the Pope himself, the Sacred Congregation for the Doctrine of the Faith, under its prefect, Joseph Cardinal Ratzinger, has released a substantial 'Instruction on Certain Aspects of the "Theology of Liberation"' (officially dated 6 August 1984). From our point of view this is a very intelligent and valuable document, as one would expect from the proven theological competence of the cardinal prefect. It fulfills the task of the congregation, which is not to intitiate great theological movements but to regulate, moderate, correct them after they have already arisen from the grass roots or the academic community. Precisely in its

---

[43] *Marx and the Bible* (Maryknoll: Orbis, 1974).

own one-sidedness it is an attempt to right the balance and to check abuses. Some of these abuses should be noted. (1) If class-struggle becomes the sovereign value, the eucharistic community could be divided along class lines, contrary to 1 Cor 11. (2) The Christian community could be turned into a political party, the priest into a politician. The transcendent, religious, spiritual aspect of the faith could be lost. Put crassly, the Vatican has a duty to see to it that the curate is there to say the eight o'clock mass, not off blowing up railroad bridges in the hills, at least not normally. (3) When liberation is identified with Marxist social theory, this can mean something like Swedish social democracy, but it can also mean something less desirable, Soviet-style one-party totalitarianism. When this happens (e.g., Cuba), not only is the last state in many ways worse than the first, but a contradiction in theory and practice arises between those Christians struggling *toward* the Soviet system (unwittingly or not) and those struggling to overthrow it (e.g., Poland). That the cardinal may himself be too closely connected with the German Christian Democratic party, or under pressure from some American business and political interests is another consideration, perhaps inseparable from the complex dialectic of human life. A point not stressed by the Instruction but by Schillebeeckx, important in this context, is that today educated Christians should not regard any political system as legitimate which does not have an actually functioning two-party pattern of power sharing.[44] Another area where further discussion needs to take place is in the understanding of sin, for the Congregation still primarily personal-individual (pre-Niebuhr), for the liberationists more social-systemic.

Because the kingdom of God is so important to liberation theology, the Instruction treats it in several places: "There is a tendency to identify the kingdom of God and its growth with the human liberation movement and to make history itself the subject of its own development as a process of the

[44] *Christ*, p. 780.

self-redemption of man by means of the class struggle (par. 9)." "One places oneself within the perspective of a temporal messianism which is one of the most radical of the expressions of secularization of the kingdom of God and of its absorption into the immanence of human history (par. 10)." "One needs to be on guard against the politicization of existence which, misunderstanding the entire meaning of the kingdom of God and the transcendence of the person, begins to sacralize politics and betray the religion of the people in favor of the projects of the revolution (par. 11)."

These statements of the Instruction have their place as prudent warnings but they do not provide the fullness of positive biblical eschatological revelation, viz., that it is precisely Jesus' message that the kingdom of God, though transcendent in origin and essence, will come to earth and to that extent become immanent, that the kingdom has social and political implications because its signs are justice and peace. Nor do this Instruction and similar documents of regional episcopates impress when they fail to mention positive achievements of this theological movement and governments influenced by it.[45]

To be sure, this biblical eschatology is still not universally accepted, not even within the biblical guild. We have mentioned Norman Perrin's ultimate hesitation (in note 1). This reserve is maintained by J.D. Crossan and the predominantly literary-aesthetic approach to the Bible. Jean Carmignac in France,[46] Hans Küng in Germany,[47] and B.D. Chilton in Britain and America[48] each in his own way

---

[45]This instruction has been followed by a second, "Instruction on Christian Freedom and Liberation" (22 March 1986). There the kingdom hope is nervously, evasively, cautiously but really affirmed in paragraphs 50, 54, 58, 60, 62, 63, 80, 99, especially in 60.

[46]"Les dangers de l'eschatologie," *NTS* 17 (1971) 365-390; *Le Mirage de l'Eschatologie* (Paris: Letouzey, 1979).

[47]Hans Küng, *Eternal Life?* (New York: Doubleday, 1985), pp. 92, 115-116, 199, 213-216, 230.

[48]*God in Strength: Jesus' Announcement of the Kingdom* (Freistadt: F. Ploechl, 1979); recently Chilton has edited an anthology of authors who try to de-eschatologize the kingdom: *The Kingdom of God in the Teaching of Jesus*

campaigns against a future apocalyptic eschatology.

As we come to the end of this brief history it might be well to glance for a moment at how someone from outside the circle of Christian faith views the matter. For the expectation of the kingdom of God is a matter of faith and hope, meaningless apart from these. Yet throughout history people have hoped for a better future and thought about the reasonableness of their hope, starting with Pandora's box in Hesiod. Today hope is again in the air, to such an extent that one of America's most learned secular minds in the area of religious studies, Morton Smith of Columbia University, has written a work called *Hope and History, an Exploration.*[49] His Yankee common sense has only pity for religious believers' expectations, yet he knows that people cannot live without hope. He does not look to God to bring a kingdom of light, but trusts only in human reason, frail as it is. As he concludes, he asks for what we can reasonably hope. He rejects any hope for final, utopian conditions, a "perfect society," as self-contradictory because it would be boring, and only change is not boring. Therefore, for Smith, hope must focus on an infinite progress, an open-ended, ongoing process, guided by human wisdom as the ability to solve new problems. He then tells this story of the Devil's wish.

> Once upon a time there was a righteous man who had three sons. The Devil hated him, but could not hurt him directly, so he tried to destroy his sons as soon as they became independent. When the eldest came of age the Devil disguised himself as a beggar and begged from him. The young man gave him a piece of money. The Devil then took the form of an angel and offered to reward him by giving him anything he wished. He wished to be king

---

(Philadelphia: Fortress, 1984). In his own contributions to this anthology, Chilton avoids the data from Daniel and Qumran, darkens council, and ignores J.A. Fitzmyer's criteria for the careful use of targums in biblical studies. For a better use of targums in kingdom research, see Klaus Koch, "Offenbaren wird sich das Reich Gottes," *NTS* 25 (1978) 158-165.

[49](New York: Harper, 1980).

and was soon murdered by a wicked courtier. When the next son came of age the Devil played the same trick. The young man wished to be rich and was soon after murdered by a robber. The third son saw what had happened to his brothers and took thought. When his turn came and the Devil made the offer, he replied, "I wish all my wishes would always come true the very moment I wished them." The Devil was bound by his promise; the wish had to be granted. The young man then wished his brothers would come back to life; the wish had to be granted. With the kingdom of the first, the wealth of the second, and the wisdom and wishes of the third, they lived happy ever after.[50]

Let us examine this story a little more closely. Smith prizes it because it teaches the lesson of the value of wisdom in coping with the ongoing problems of life rather than the lure of a final solution. But the story betrays its bourgeois sensibility in that it presupposes conditions of justice and peace. (The father of the sons is described a righteous.) Moreover, the first two sons want a kingdom and prosperity. A kingdom can be godly when it is just and peaceful and its citizens prosper. But it can also be a realm of oppression, domination, exploitation and cruelty. Thus the story could be understood as expressing a longing for the kingdom of God supposing the sons to be as righteous as their father. In this context the third wish for the wisdom to cope with the unknowns of the future does not contradict but complements the longing for God's kingdom which is indeed said in Daniel to be without end. But this wisdom would not need to fear the future within the kingdom because the basic conditions in which wisdom can best flourish, justice and peace, would already have been guaranteed. These conditions do not yet prevail in the world. That is why millions still feel they must pray, "Thy kingdom come."

[50] *Hope and History*, pp. 218f.

CONCLUSION

In this work, at once a chronicle of the history of an idea and a report on the periodic eruption of this idea into the world of history, we have attempted first of all to determine the original meaning of the central message of Jesus' preaching. This we found to be the near arrival of the kingdom of God in the sense of a new, future divine breaking into history, already present in sign, anticipation and momentary ecstasy, especially in the ministry of Jesus himself, yet in its fullness still to come. This divine act will be of a social rather than an individual character and will have as its immediate political manifestations justice and peace. As well it will involve a new and greater outpouring of God's Holy Spirit upon those who enter this kingdom.

Once Jesus had sealed this proclamation with his death on the cross and, as believers hold, had received the divine confirmation of his preaching through his being raised from the dead, his message of hope enjoyed a varied fortune. Still alive in Paul, it recedes in the gospel according to John before the promise of eternal life. After that it flickers on fitfully in its original sense in the early church fathers and apologists and enjoys a brief flowering in St. Irenaeus.

We then discerned three other main patterns or types of kingdom understanding emerging in the life of the patristic, medieval and early modern periods. These are the spiritual-mystical-celestial pattern of Origen and other Platonizing theologians; the Christian imperial pattern of Eusebius, Constantine and later emperors and court theologians; the ecclesial interpretation of Augustine and other churchmen. With the Anabaptists a proletarian revolutionary attempt at realizing the kingdom appears on the scene. With Kant the kingdom is understood as an ethical commonwealth which for all practical purposes is built by man. In this golden era of the Social Gospel one missionary complained that every time he attended a lecture on modern missions and the kingdom of God it turned out to be a talk on how to improve chicken breeding among the natives. This has its value but is not the fullness of revelation. With Weiss, Schweitzer and Barth the kingdom once again becomes God's to build and to bring, but we can prepare the way for it and perhaps hasten its coming by removing the obstacles to it. Like John the Baptist we can point to and prepare for the work of God even though we do not identify our efforts, which often fail and are sometimes misguided, with his great work, the kingdom.

With Jürgen Moltmann exegesis, systematics and philosophy of history converge in centering the hope of humanity on the kingdom of God.

The problems that arise in neo-Kantian moralism, Social Gospel and liberation theology can all be reduced theologically to the problem of Pelagianism, the idea that we save ourselves, that our efforts are the will and work of God *tout court*, that we build the kingdom directly ourselves. Such a view does not allow God to be God, sovereign lord and free to do greater good than we can ask or imagine. A sane theology of the divine-human encounter must allow a place for the human ethical response. The Scriptures are full of this kind of exhortation. But the value of our response must not be overestimated. If salvation depended on ourselves alone many would despair. Experience of history and faith teach us that if there is a force working for justice it must be greater than ourselves. "Only a god can save us" (Heidegger).

Traditionally Ignatius of Loyola has been quoted as saying, "Pray as if everything depended on God. Work as if everything on you." Recent research has shown that what Ignatius actually wrote was, "Pray as if everything depended upon yourself. Work as if everything depended upon God," a subtler teaching.

Biblical exegesis of the kingdom theme cannot solve all our problems or give us specific political programs. But it can point us in the right direction in the quest for social justice. (1) Once we see how much God still cares for this tired old world, we learn to expect more in this world, in life, in time and history. We learn to hope again. (2) We learn to take this world seriously. Christian hope includes not only the resurrection and eternal life with God in heaven but also the kingdom of God on earth. (3) We learn to engage in the struggle for justice and a humane social order and peace (disarmament) without illusion (no purely human program will bring in the kingdom of God) and without despair, because God is faithful to his promise and he will bring in his kingdom.

FOR FURTHER READING

FOR FURTHER READING

I. The Kingdom in the Old Testament
and Intertestamental Period

Bright, John, *The Kingdom of God* (Nashville: Abingdon, 1950).

Buber, Martin, *The Kingship of God* (New York: Harper, 1967).

Collins, J.J., *Daniel, First Maccabees, Second Maccabees with an Excusus on the Apocalyptic Genre* (Wilmington: Glazier, 1981), and the literature there cited.

Gray, John, *The Biblical Doctrine of the Reign of God* (Edinburgh: Clark, 1979).

Russell, D.S., *Apocalyptic Ancient and Modern* (Philadelphia: Fortress, 1978).

Camponovo, Odo, *Königtum, Königsherrschaft und Reich Gottes in den frühjüdischen Schriften* (Fribourg: Universitätsverlag, 1984).

II. The Kingdom of God in the New Testament

Weiss, Johannes, *Jesus' Proclamation of the Kingdom of God* (Philadelphia: Fortress, 1971; orig. 1892).

Schweitzer, Albert, *The Quest of the Historical Jesus* (New York: Macmillan, 1969; orig. 1906).

The two works just mentioned were the classics which inaugurated the modern study of the theme. Two histories of research follow:

Perrin, Norman, *The Kingdom of God in the Teaching of Jesus* (Philadelphia: Westminster, 1963).

Lundström, Gösta, *The Kingdom of God in the Teaching of Jesus* (London: Oliver and Boyd, 1963).

Schnackenburg, Rudolf, *God's Rule and Kingdom* (New York: Herder & Herder, 1963; orig. 1959). A model of thoroughness, the most balanced treatment of all the biblical data, non-partisan.

Perrin, Norman, *Jesus and the Language of the Kingdom: Symbol and Metaphor in New Testament Interpretation* (Philadelphia: Fortress, 1976). As the subtitle suggests, this book represents a shift in understanding of the kingdom which makes it a symbol without the hope of a future act of God in history.

Four dissertation books follow:

Hiers, R.H., *The Kingdom of God in the Synoptic Tradition* (Gainesville: University of Florida, 1970); *The Historical Jesus and the Kingdom of God* (Gainesville: University of Florida, 1973).

Kelber, Werner, *The Kingdom of God in Mark* (Philadelphia: Fortress, 1974).

Ambrozic, A.M., *The Hidden Kingdom: ___ The Kingdom of God in Mark's Gospel* (Washington, D.C.: The Catholic Biblical Association of America, 1972).

Schlosser, Jacques, *Le Règne de Dieu dans les Dits de Jésus* (Paris: Gabalda, 1980).

Some recent articles:

Koch, Klaus, "Offenbaren wird sich das Reich Gottes," *New Testament Studies* 25 (1979) 158-166.

Légasse, Simon, "Le retour du Christ d'après l'évangile de Jean: chapitres 14 et 16: une adaptation du motif de la Parousie," *Bulletin de Littérature Ecclésiastique* 81 (1980) 161-174.

Pamment, Margaret, "The Kingdom of Heaven According to the First Gospel," *New Testament Studies* 27 (1981) 211-232.

Walker, W.O., "The Kingdom of the Son of Man and the Kingdom of the Father in Matthew," *Catholic Biblical Quarterly* 30 (1968) 573-579.

Wilder, Amos, *Kerygma, Eschatology and Social Ethics* (Philadelphia: Fortress, 1966).

Chilton, Bruce, ed., *The Kingdom of God* (Philadelphia: Fortress, 1984). An anthology of readings, somewhat tendentiously edited, but some articles are worthwhile, e.g., that by Lattke.

Merklein, Helmut, *Die Gottesherrschaft als Handlungsprinzip. Untersuchung zur Ethik Jesu* (Würzburg: Echter, 1978).

Aalen, Sverre, "Reign and House in the Kingdom of God in the Gospels," *New Testament Studies* 8 (1961-2) 215-240. On the question of the territorial nature of the kingdom.

E.P. Sanders, *Jesus and Judaism* (Philadelphia: Fortress, 1985), pp. 123-156, 222-241, a recent, accurate study.

III. The Kingdom of God in Patristic Theology

Frick, R., *Die Geschichte des Reich-Gottes-Gedankens in der alten Kirche bis zu Origenes und Augustin* (Giessen: Töpelmann, 1928).

Lampe, G.W.H., "Some notes on the significance of *basileia tou theou, basileia christou,* in the Greek Fathers," *Journal of Theological Studies* 49 (1948) 58-73.

Barnard, L.W., "Justin Martyr's Eschatology," *Vigiliae Christianae* 19 (1965) 86-98.

Grant, R.M., *Early Christianity and Society* (San Francisco: Harper, 1977).

Jones, A.H.M., *Constantine and the Conversion of Europe* (Harmondsworth: Penguin, 1962).

Markus, R.A., *Saeculum: History and Society in the Theology of St. Augustine* (Cambridge: University Press, 1970).

Versfeld, Marthinus, *A Guide to the City of God* (New York: Sheed and Ward, 1958).

Of course, the most important thing is to read the Fathers themselves, particularly the Apostolic Fathers, Justin Martyr, Irenaeus, and Augustine, whose *City of God*, esp. Books 18-20, is the major patristic treatment of the theme. General surveys of the theology of the period include those by Danielou, Pelikan and Bouyer.

IV. The Kingdom of God in the Middle Ages

Reeves, Marjorie, *The Influence of Prophecy in the Later Middle Ages* (Oxford: Clarendon, 1969).

Reeves, Marjorie, *Joachim of Fiore and the Prophetic Future* (New York: Harper, 1976).

McGinn, Bernard, *Apocalyptic Spirituality* (New York: Paulist, 1979).

McGinn, Bernard, *Visions of the End* (New York: Columbia, 1979).

de Lubac, Henri, *Exégèse Mediévale,* vol. 3, (Paris: Aubier, 1961).

de Lubac, Henri, *La Posterité de Joachim de Flore* (Paris: Lethielleux, 1979).

Dempf, Alois, *Sacrum Imperium* (Munich-Berlin: R. Oldenburg, 1929: repr. 1973).

Kantorowicz, Ernst, *Laudes Regiae: A Study in Liturgical Acclamations and Medieval Ruler Worship* (Berkeley: University of California, 1946).

Ratzinger, Joseph, *The Theology of History in St. Bonaventure* (Chicago: Franciscan Herald, 1971; German orig. 1959).

Schachten, H.J., *Ordo Salutis: Das Gesetz als Reise der Heilsvermittlung. Zur Kritik des hl. Thomas von Aquin an Joachim von Fiore* (Münster: Aschendorff, 1980).

Seckler, Max, *Das Heil in der Geschichte. Geschichtstheologisches Denken bei Thomas von Aquin* (Munich: Kösel, 1964).

Mottu, Henri, *La Manifestation de l'Esprit selon Joachim de Fiore* (Neuchâtel-Paris: Delachaux et Niestlé, 1977).

V. The Kingdom of God in Modern Thought

Niebuhr, H.R., *The Kingdom of God in America* (New York: Scribners, 1937).

Braaten, Carl, *The Future of God: The Revolutionary Dynamics of Hope* (New York: Harper, 1969).

Davis, Charles, *Theology and Political Society* (Cambridge: University Press, 1980).

Gilkey, Langdon, *Reaping the Whirlwind: A Christian Interpretation of History* (New York: Seabury, 1976).

Hertz, K.H., ed., *Two Kingdoms and One World* (Minneapolis: Augsburg, 1976).

Löwith, Karl, *Meaning in History* (Chicago: University of Chicago, 1949).

Ludger, G. and T. Michels, ed., *Reich Gottes-Kirche-Civitas Dei* (Salzburg: Otto Müller, 1981).

Metz, J.B., *Followers of Christ* (New York: Paulist, 1977).

Miranda, José, *Marx and the Bible* (New York: Orbis, 1971).

Moltmann, Jürgen, *The Theology of Hope* (New York: Haprer, 1967).

Moltmann, Jürgen, *The Experiment Hope* (Philadelphia: Fortress, 1975).

Moltmann, Jürgen, *The Trinity and the Kingdom of God* (New York: Harper, 1980).

Newbigin, Lesslie, *Sign of the Kingdom* (Grand Rapids: Eerdmans, 1980).

Pannenberg, Wolfhart, ed., *Revelation as History* (London: Macmillan, 1961).

Pannenberg, Wolfhart, *Theology and the Kingdom of God* (Philadelphia: Westminster, 1969).

Rottenberg, I.C., *The Promise and the Presence: Toward a Theology of the Kingdom of God* (Grand Rapids: Eerdmans, 1980).

Schindler, Alfred, *Monotheismus als politisches Problem? Erik Peterson und die Kritik der politische Theologie* (Gütersloh: Mohn, 1978).

Smith, Morton, *Hope and History: An Exploration* (New York: Harper, 1980).

Tillich, Paul, *The Socialist Decision* (New York: Harper, 1977; orig. 1933).

Tillich, Paul, *Systematic Theology* (Chicago: University of Chicago, 1963), vol. 3, pp. 297-423.

INDEX

INDEX OF
SCRIPTURE REFERENCES

INDEX OF NAMES